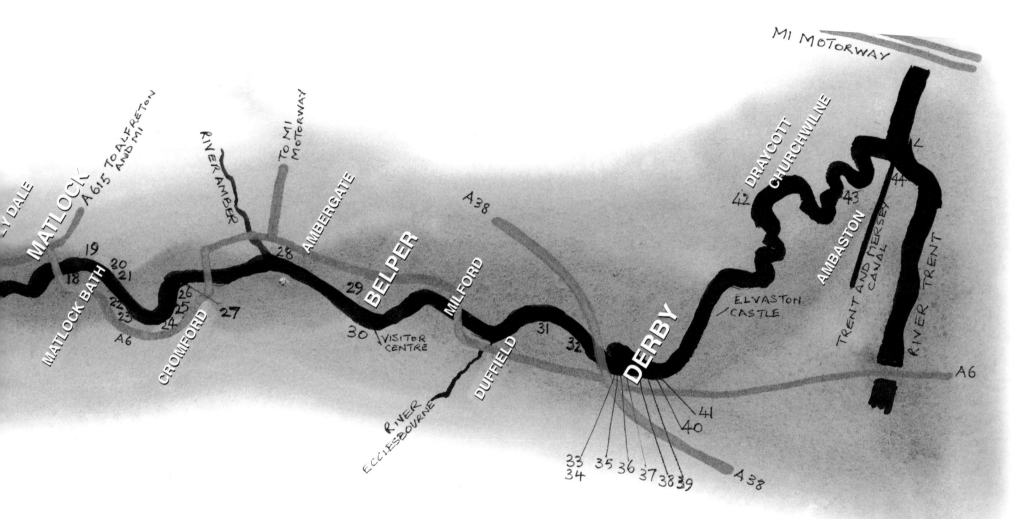

Riverside Journey

A Portrait of the Derwent

For Diana

Riverside Journey

A Portrait of the Derwent

ASHLEY BRYANT

The Lutterworth Press
Cambridge

First Published in 2001 by:
The Lutterworth Press
P.O. Box 60
Cambridge
CB1 2NT
England

e-mail: **publishing@lutterworth.com**
website: **http://www.lutterworth.com**

ISBN 0 7188 3013 X

British Library Cataloguing in Publication Data:
A catalogue record is available from the British Library.

Printed in China

INTRODUCTION

The Derwent flows through a landscape offering unrivalled beauty and variety, and this book has offered an exciting challenge in presenting its progress in a series of paintings. Rising in high moorland it tumbles along a steep sided valley dropping a thousand feet in six miles to reach 'Lakeland Derbyshire', a chain of distinctive reservoirs with conifer-clad valley sides and moorland heights. A series of gritstone edges takes us towards the limestone gorge of Matlock. Gritstone edges on the eastern side continue to Baslow, and one example, Curbar Edge, is shown in the paintings on page 11. The middle range of the River encounters the limestone gorge at Matlock, introducing some of the most spectacular scenery in Britain and eliciting praise from poets such as Byron who compared this with 'anything as fair in Greece or Switzerland'. The valley, now more gentle and thickly wooded, takes us towards the northern outskirts of Derby from which the River flows lazily over a wide flood plain to join the Trent after a journey of 66 miles.

The Derwent experiences a wide variety of geographical conditions, which in turn introduce a variety of different habitats for wildlife, providing a diverse range of flora and fauna along its length. On windswept moorland 2000 feet above sea level, near the River's source, heather, grasses and various berry bushes survive the harsh environment, but as the River tumbles down its steep valley trees and copses emerge. Extensive conifer forests planted around the reservoirs give way to deciduous woodlands and ultimately a rich agricultural valley as the River flows through Derby and on to the Trent.

The high moorlands are home to mountain hares – one of the few places in Britain where they are found outside Scotland – and endangered raptors like the merlin and hen harrier are present here. Goshawks are resident around the reservoirs, the woods also support crossbills and redpoll, and on the dark, brooding reservoirs themselves an osprey will make an appearance once in a while. The Derwent valley is particularly favoured by the pied flycatcher and newcomers like the goosander have colonised the River enthusiastically. I don't want to dwell here too much on individual species, but it is encouraging to note the otter is making a welcome return, and hopefully this may be followed by salmon in the not too distant future.

The swift flow of the Derwent prompted a number of cotton mills to be constructed in the last third of the eighteenth century and these played a major part in shaping the industrial revolution. Key individuals like Arkwright and Strutt were leaders in harnessing water power for cotton spinning, and started the industrialisation of the Derwent Valley, which has developed and diversified over two hundred years. The valley is now regarding with such interest by historians that World Heritage Status has been proposed for the section of the River from Cromford to Derby, and its prospects look encouraging. Cotton spinning, however, was found over much of the Derwent, and its swift waters have driven mills for various purposes for many centuries.

Villages and towns add interest, history and character to the progress of the Derwent, and for the artist their old bridges, riverside buildings and colourful customs provide a rich diversity of subjects. One of the finest country houses in Britain is situated by the River at Chatsworth where the Derwent flows through a Capability Brown parkland. The estate village of Edensor, with its striking architecture, contrasts sharply with the worker village at Cromford where Arkwright built functional, stone houses for his mill workers.

Recently an organisation known as the Derwent Valley Trust has been introduced, with the objective of promoting the beauty and heritage of the Derwent Valley as an important natural asset. Another aspect of the Trust's activity is the Heritage Way, a long-distance footpath which is being developed to take the visitor by riverside paths from the reservoirs in the north to Elvaston Castle near Derby in the south.

My project to record the Derwent in this series of paintings has taken more than three years and has necessitated many visits and many miles of walking along its delightful banks. In some instances I have visited the same locations several times in order to appreciate the changes that are brought about by different seasons. Sometimes I have been unlucky with the weather, but another occasion has offered a glorious day to make the scene sparkle.

A question I am often asked is 'Do you prefer watercolours or oils?' My answer offends neither camp as I really don't mind which medium I use. For me, the interest of painting lies in developing the subject with emphasis on content, focus, depth, lighting and atmosphere, whilst the mechanics and techniques of the medium are not important issues. Having made this point, most of the colour reproductions in this book are watercolours. For my field sketches I normally use charcoal, which is fast and fluent, and some of these, even some which have taken a few minutes, are reproduced here and these contrast with the carefully worked-out watercolours.

Another question often posed at exhibitions is 'Isn't it difficult to part with them?' It is true there is sometimes a considerable wrench when they are sold, since a great deal of work and thought goes into them. No artist can produce a painting any other way. It is therefore natural with so much of your life-force and creativity behind your work to feel sad when you part with them. This book is the logical conclusion where these paintings can be kept together as a complete record, but also as an opportunity to present some of my experiences in visiting the Derwent and to record aspects of this fascinating river.

There I sat viewing the silver streams glide silently towards their centre, the tempestuous sea; yet sometimes opposed by rugged roots and pebble-stones, which broke their waves and turned them into foam. . . . As I thus sat, these and other sights had so fully possessed my soul with content, that I thought, as the poet hath happily expressed it,

> I was for that time lifted above earth,
> And possess'd joys not promised in my birth.

Izaak Walton, *The Compleat Angler*

1. THE SOURCE

Ever since my teenage days I have enjoyed walking in the Peak District and over a period of forty years I have covered much of Kinder and Bleaklow. However, I must confess that I had never stood next to the first trickle of water and said 'That's the very spot where the Derwent begins.'

It therefore felt like an expedition a few years ago years ago when I set out, accompanied by two of my sons and a good friend and fellow walker, from Howden Reservoir to discover the source of the Derwent. You can approach the Derwent's headland from the A628 which lies two miles to the north, but you may prefer the excitement of walking the last few miles upstream, following the River into an increasingly wild and lonely landscape of high moorland. And lonely it is – I have walked this area several times since then and hardly seen another soul. Providing you are fit and a reasonably experienced walker I can recommend the circular route by following the River upstream from Howden Reservoir, then returning via Ridgewalk Moor and the River Westend, which flows into a spur to the reservoir's western side, a distance of twelve miles. On weekdays you can conveniently leave your car at the north end of Howden Reservoir, but the road is closed at weekends.

On reaching the River's head in an area marked on the map between Swain's Head and Swain's Greave you find that the actual source of the Derwent is open to interpretation. Hills to the north, west and south act like giant sponges soaking up rainfall and draining into a marshy basin, from which the River flows continuously, marking for some people the Derwent's source. It is small enough to step across but it has an energy and determination that is seen in the lovely River we are about to follow.

However, an alternative consideration sets the Derwent's source back a little further. Drainage into the basin is assisted by a radiating network of gullies that remain dry much of the time but which cascade down the hillsides in wet weather. The longest of these can be acknowledged as the Derwent's ultimate stretch and if we follow this to its origin we emerge on the edge of a moorland plateau over 1900 feet high, a few hundred yards south west of the Barrow Stones, a prominent rock outcrop. The scramble up this gully is rewarded with spectacular long-distance views to the north and north east. I've sat here several times admiring the view with racing clouds casting fast moving shadows over the landscape, the wind whipping round my ears and blowing the coffee from my flask as I pour a celebration cup. It's quite a trek up here but worth all the effort and it is an unforgettable experience.

The painting tries to encompass as many of the characteristics of this area as possible. The view looks southwards about two hundred yards up towards the summit on a lovely August day. The gully is dry with a pool of peaty water in a boulder-strewn bed whilst steeply eroded sides and short wind-blown vegetation complete the picture. The weather on Bleaklow can change quickly, and ten minutes into a sudden downpour would convert this scene into a torrent of water racing through a grey mist. Fortunately our day remained fair and this charcoal sketch shows my band of tired but intrepid explorers admiring the view.

The Derwent's origin in this beautiful upland scenery is impressive indeed, and its isolation even more amazing when you consider how close we are to Manchester and Sheffield. As we shall see the River continues to give us delight, interest and a few surprises on its way south to the Trent.

Admiring the view

2. BLEAK WINTER

Few people venture over Bleaklow in Winter; the very name makes you shiver, but if you are well organised and prepared, it can be an exhilarating experience. The Derwent is barely half a mile from its source in this painting and seen after a heavy fall of snow – not unusual here.

In my late teens I had a very lucky escape in this Winter's landscape when I entered a long distance endurance race across fifty miles of the most difficult sections of the Peak District. Our team of three trained for months beforehand, tackling marathon-sized sections of the route each week, building up super-fitness and knowledge of landmarks and compass bearings. Although the event had always been held in mid March, the weather had always been good in previous years.

We set out at dawn from Holmfirth in Yorkshire, fit as fiddles and utterly determined, despite a cold drizzle which soon turned to rain. It had rained all the previous week and our first major ascent over Blackhills was through knee-high bog. Despite this we kept our schedules, resolute and enthusiastic. On the climb up Bleaklow the rain turned to snow and then on the tops we met the full force of a blizzard that reduced visibility to almost nil. This necessitated walking with the compass constantly to hand, inching mile after mile across the landscape, the gullies building up with deep drifts of snow and making progress even more precarious.

We were soaked through to the skin and very cold; any movement other than the slow rhythm of walking was difficult. Our kit had been pruned to the minimum in the interests of speed – standard practise then – and I only wore a thin shirt under a lightweight, non-waterproof anorak. We had no rations or emergency supplies.

After several miles we suddenly lost our compass bearer. We called and searched, then yelled in vain – he had simply disappeared in the blizzard. Ultimately we continued in grim despair, knowing we would freeze if we waited another minute. On reaching a small valley we decided to follow it downwards – without a compass or knowledge of our position this was our only solution. Eventually the valley side became so steep that we had to cross over to the other side, but the trickle of water we would normally have expected had turned into a river of icy water pounding down the boulder-strewn bed. I fell into the racing torrent of water and was swept down about fifty yards before my companion could rescue me. None the wetter, but with all reserves of warmth depleted, I soon started to lose my balance – an odd feeling, which worsened to the extent that I eventually had to crawl. FInally, just as I lost consciousness, I had a feeling of warmth and comfort – as if in a dream.

I awoke in a Land Rover on the way to hospital – fortunately with our lost colleague who had also been rescued. I still have the press cutting from that day recording the death of one competitor and the search for two others who did not survive.

The whole system was radically changed afterwards with essential controls and safety measures, but it was a very close shave, and had I been a cat one of my nine lives would definitely have been ticked off! Our next views of the Derwent fortunately take us to warmer times.

Blizzard on Bleaklow

3. PEATY POOLS

About a mile and a half from the source of the River we find these delightful pools with a series of small waterfalls cascading down into the pool beneath. This is a lovely place to sit awhile and reflect on the beauty of the upper Derwent in its sheltered valley away from the bustling crowds. But you soon realise that you are not really alone. . .

Looking in the heather we see all kinds of life. Beetles of various descriptions, spiders crawling in the branches and small moths struggling through the compacted heather to fly off into the daylight. There is certainly a sufficient insect population to support an interesting variety of bird life on these moors.

The most common bird is the meadow pipit, brown and sparrow sized with white stripes down the side of its tail. Oddly enough you are likely to see cuckoos here in the Spring and early Summer, since they like to lay their eggs in meadow pipit's nests. It's not unusual to watch a cuckoo being chased by an irate meadow pipit at this time of the year.

There's nothing more appealing than the strange warbling sound of the curlew, an evocative sound floating over the air from some distance, welcoming but mournful, uplifting yet hypnotic. Golden plovers are much at home here too, as well as the ring ousel, and you may see the occasional whinchat or wheatear.

In addition to heather, moorland grasses and sedges, there are patches of bracken, cotton grass on boggy areas and several types of low growing berry bushes on these moors, the most unusual of which is cloudberry. Its name is derived from the fact that it prefers damp, misty conditions, and likes to keep its 'head in the clouds' but it is rare to find one bearing berries in this region, the southern extent of its range.

In the 1870s and 1880s mountain hares were introduced into the Peak District from Scotland, and have fared well, especially in recent mild Winters. They develop white coats in Winter, moulting in the Spring to their blue-grey appeerance, hence their alternative name of blue hare.

On one occasion I spotted an adder snaking along the path but as soon as it moved into the heather its zig-zag markings of brown and yellow rendered it invisible. I had always thought they were creatures of southern heathlands but they flourish well enough on the cold Derbyshire moors.

The bird that has the greatest impact, especially when one springs up at your feet, is the red grouse. You jump out of your skin as it suddenly bursts into the air with its loud 'kek kek kek' alarm call – often when you are least expecting it. It is these very birds that help to preserve the moorland status; indeed we refer to these areas as 'grouse' moors. Much of this area is maintained for grouse shooting and without the grouse the moorland environment would degenerate through lack of management – the heather would grow old and woody, bracken and gorse would invade, and the whole natural balance would change, denying us those magnificent vistas of flowering purple heather.

Merlin in pursuit

Ashley Bryant

4. MOORLAND VALLEY

From Humber Knolls along Lands Side the path moves away from the River on to the high slopes and affords magnificent views of the valley with Howden Moors climbing to our left and Ronksley Moor over to the right. We are now about three miles from the source on our southward treck.

The Derwent follows a text-book example of a river, rising in high country, its swift flowing water creating a 'V' shaped valley, then as it slows slightly it develops a 'U' shaped valley and finally as a slow meandering mature river it carves out a wide flood plain. In reality nothing is quite so simple, and the Derwent occasionally repeats and even reverses the established rules. As we look down to the River even at this early stage we see the first instance of a meander in a flat bottomed valley but the River is soon off again with gusto carving out a steep-sided route towards the reservoirs.

In this region the first hardy trees start to appear, growing lower down the valley sides where they receive a little more protection from the biting winter winds. Rowan, birch and sessile oaks pave the way, and a further mile or two downstream we reach Oaken Bank which lives up to its name as the trees form a small copse on the hillside. This area is ideal territory for another type of pipit – the tree pipit, which prefers a moorland or heathland habitat with occasional trees. It is an unmistakable bird – at least when it sings. It launches itself from the highest branch in its domain, flies upwards to its chosen height then descends with wings fluttering in a frenzy of twittering.

There are some rare species of bird you may just be lucky enough to observe as the habitat in this painting is ideal for them. Merlins nest here, but these, our smallest falcons, are in decline as a result of loss of habitat nationwide.

Merlins tend to keep watch from rocks or clumps of heather and are difficult to spot; the most likely sighting is when they are chasing their lunch. Hen harriers occasionally breed on these moors and have a more visible presence with their slow moth-like flight, the male being very striking with his grey and black plumage. A more common raptor on these moors is the short-eared owl, and owing to their habit of hunting during the day you may spot one. Good luck!

The moors above the valley present a windswept and inhospitable environment today but there is evidence of past human activity and settlement. The original tree cover of sessile oak, birch, rowan and wych elm was cut down and regeneration prevented by grazing. Numerous ancient tracks cross the moors and there are some tumuli and sacred sites.

Ring Ousel

5. BY CRANBERRY BED

A mile or so below Oaken Bank the valley opens out and we reach an area where the Derwent is more accessible. Here you can walk by its banks along sheep-grazed rough pasture and enjoy the pace and flow of the stream with its rills and waterfalls.

As a child I would have loved to be able to wade in these pools and spent hours making dams with the abundant building materials. There is clear evidence that children still enjoy this pastime and I'm sure a picnic here on a Summer's day would long remain a pleasant memory.

Although we have descended nearly 1000 feet from the source of the Derwent the climate is still harsh, and the painting I produced of this stretch was based on the conditions at the end of the first week of May. You may think it looks more like March or even a damp November day; new Spring grass has not yet really made an appearance and the young bracken plants that clothe the area in Summer are still dormant. Several miles south bluebells are flowering and warblers are singing, but here the full thrust of Spring is delayed.

This painting shows the Derwent looking north along Cranberry Bed at the location where the brook along Cranberry Clough enters the River. The name is of course derived from the cranberry which flourishes here, along with other species of berries, as familiar moorland plants.

There are good walks around this area and I have often recommended the short walk up Cranberry Clough to meet a footpath that runs southwards parallel to the valley, then descends over Upper Hey and Howden Clough to Howden reservoir, returning via the pine woods along the Derwent.

Strolling along this stretch one day I was aware of another walker behind me with whom I talked when he passed me. He told me he had retired as a doctor 15 years ago and came here every Friday to walk in the area. He loved it – different routes, different weather conditions and changes of season gave every visit a variety and he clearly thrived on the exercise. Our paths eventually parted and he strode up his hill in a manner which made a mockery of his advanced years!

A somewhat different experience happened to me a few years ago when I stayed in a guest house in the High Peak with some walking friends. There were several old ladies there – apparently holding a re-union from their days as fellow teachers. They had kitted themselves out in various anoraks and boots and appeared to be keenly looking forward to a day's walking. We were very impressed. It transpired that they only walked 50 yards into the garden where they enjoyed a sumptuous picnic. If I can walk like the doctor or enjoy myself like those ladies when I am in my 80s I will be well pleased!

If we take a backward glance at this stage, we see the Derwent descending from the Bleaklow hills, providing an endless opportunity for artistic inspiration. The small painting on this page of the little waterfall along Cranberry bed is but one example, but it's time to move downstream for one more painting before the reservoirs.

The Waterfall

Ashley Bryant

6. THE FIRST BRIDGE

This could equally be entitled 'The Last Bridge' depending on your viewpoint, but clearly it is the most northerly bridge over the Derwent and just a few yards from Cranberry Clough at a location called 'Slippery Stones'. The delightfully proportioned but robust structure seems at odds with its function as a hikers' bridge, but it was originally built as a packhorse bridge in the eighteenth century where it graced the village of Derwent. Prior to the flooding of the valley to create the reservoirs the end arches of the bridge were dismantled and rebuilt here in 1959 about half a mile north of Howden Reservoir. It provides a physical link with the submerged village of Derwent.

The slopes around the valley are cloaked in softwoods of sitka spruce, pine and larch. You may sometimes come across a birdwatcher or two, they tend to be seen in pairs. With more than my fair share of curiosity I have sometimes asked what they are looking at through their telescopes and binoculars. The answer is often goshawks – at least they hope to see one. For two hundred years these large grey hawks with their barred plumage and penetrating eyes have been persecuted to the point of extinction, but in recent years have staged a come-back. They prefer remote areas of large woodland and seem well suited to the forests around the reservoirs. They are shy birds though, and the chance of seeing one is slim as they keep well hidden and their movements are cautious. The last birdwatchers I talked with, a man-and-wife team, had spent a two-day vigil without success; nevertheless their enthusiasm was undiminished and they expected to see one at any moment. I left them thinking that birdwatchers and fishermen have a lot in common!

To many people including myself, the 'first bridge' represents a significant milestone; to the north are some of the wildest and most remote parts of the Peak District. One walker I met said she felt like a hobbit from Tolkien's *Lord of the Rings* when she crossed this bridge, as though she was venturing from the 'Shire' into the wilderness beyond. This point certainly represents a gateway to the wild and lonely countryside in the upper reaches of the River.

With snow on the ground it is not always possible to reach some of these areas in the Upper Derwent Valley; the difficulty is more associated with access by car to your starting point than the actual difficulty of walking across a snow-covered landscape. (At least as an artist you can add a little more snow to a painting – so long as you have renewed your artist's licence.) On this occasion, the weather was really cold as I sketched the scene, precariously close to the water's edge.

The River now carves out a steep valley as it plunges down towards the upper reaches of Howden reservoir, finally cutting a fast-flowing stony bed through the trees. It's the nearest you will get to British Columbia or Vancouver on the eastern side of the Atlantic, and – if you have a good imagination – you can see the grizzly bears as they stand in mid-stream to catch the salmon!

Ashley Bryant

7. HOWDEN RESERVOIR

At the end of the Victorian era the growing cities of Sheffield and the east Midlands required increasing water supplies, and to satisfy this demand two large reservoirs were eventually constructed in the upper Derwent Valley. The first one, Howden Reservoir, was constructed between 1901 and 1912, and downstream the Derwent Reservoir was built between 1902 and 1916. With some foresight, a railway line was constructed along the valley sides so that the vast quantity of stone could be transported to construct the castellated dams, now regarded as a feature of this 'lakeland' part of the Peak District.

A worker's village nicknamed 'Tintown' was created at Birchinlee to house the many people needed for this project. Unlike the unruly 'navvies' who terrorised the countryside during the building of the canals and railways a hundred years earlier these workers were closely supervised, and a list of stringent regulations at the site of this settlement makes interesting reading!

The reservoirs certainly give the area an attractive landscape feature, but I would have liked to have witnessed the valley before the flooding, and followed the Derwent as it twisted and tumbled along its majestic course. The River Westend, a tributary of the Derwent, creates a major spur to Howden Reservoir and I'm sure this area would have kept me painting for weeks with its inspirational scenery.

The steep sides of the valley were planted with a monoculture of conifers which has become dark and depressing on maturity, but fortunately beech and other deciduous trees have been planted around the edges and by the reservoir roads to soften the appearance. Several unusual bird species can be found in these steeply sloping woodlands. I have already noted the goshawk, but its smaller cousin the sparrowhawk can be seen here too. Two uncommon finches, the redpoll and crossbill are ideally adapted to life in these conifer forests, and the pied flycatcher makes itself known – in fact this species is seen along a long stretch of the Derwent having successfully bred over several decades, providing one of the highest populations in Britain of this uncommon bird. Nesting boxes have helped its breeding success.

This view looks north east from a spur of land on the western side – near to the top end of Howden Reservoir. It is late April and billowing clouds give the strong possibility of yet another April shower.

Moving downstream beyond Howden Dam and Derwent Dam we come to the Fairholmes Visitor Centre where a large totem pole, carved with images of local wildlife, attracts a great deal of attraction. The Visitor Centre also supports the friendliest ducks, geese and sheep, which willingly share your sandwiches, and chaffinches so tame they will sit on your hand to take crumbs.

Downstream at the Fairholmes Visitor Centre

Ashley Bryant

8. DERWENT DAM

As demand for water continued to increase, work on a third reservoir started in the 1930s. Unlike Howden and Derwent Reservoirs which affected only a few isolated farms, the new Ladybower Reservoir swallowed up two whole villages – Derwent and Ashopton.

Derwent lay in the valley near the present Bridge-End car park, a small community of around 60 people; with the impressive Jacobean Derwent Hall and its ornamental lake and attractive grounds. Before the valley was flooded most of the buildings were demolished, the church tower being left as a sort of monument, only to be blown up in 1947. As previously mentioned, the ends of the lovely packhorse bridge across the River were saved and rebuilt at Slippery Stones. When the water is low, remains of this village can still be seen as a rather sad reminder of a lost community.

The second village to be submerged was the larger and more bustling Ashopton, sited at the southern side of the present Ashopton viaduct which takes the Sheffield to Glossop road across Ladybower Reservoir. Old photos show construction of this lofty viaduct – now all that can be seen is the top section as the waters lap near the undersides of the arches, an indication of how deep Ashopton lies buried beneath the waters, its houses, streets, post office and once busy coaching inn preserved for ever in a layer of silt.

A practical measure to assist the building of the reservoirs was the construction of a railway line from Bamford to Birchinlee (the site of the worker village) to transport the vast amount of stone required for construction of the dams, and the present road along the reservoirs largely follows this route. Remains of the temporary wooden railway viaduct across the Ashop Valley can still be seen at low water.

The reservoirs were used during the second world war to train fighter pilots of 617 Squadron in dropping 'bouncing bombs' to breach the Möhne and Eder dams of the Ruhr valley in Germany. The 'Dam Busters', the now-classic 1950s film of their exploit, was filmed in the Derwent Valley.

Whilst most people see the reservoirs from the road on the western side of the valley, the most interesting views are enjoyed from walks around the valley sides and tops. A stroll along Derwent Edge on the eastern flank affords spectacular views from prominent rock outcrops such as the Salt Cellar – an eroded gritstone landmark. On the opposite side, Win Hill provides a magnificent vantage point, as well as a feeling of achievement when you reach the summit!

The acid soils and high rainfall of the area provide ideal conditions for rhodedendrons and you will never see healthier specimens than around these reservoirs. There magnificent blooms inspired me to paint this picture as we scan the Gothic outlines of Derwent Dam. This lakeland scenery encourages the artist to dwell further, but there are new and interesting horizons awaiting us as we move downstream from the Upper Derwent Valley.

Evening on Derwent Edge

Ashley Bryant

9. PICNIC AT LEADMILL BRIDGE

From the reservoirs the Derwent flows past Bamford where the most northerly cotton mill was constructed on the River, then on past the village of Hathersage where a magnificent valley unfolds. Just upstream of the village, stepping stones provide a rather risky crossing of the River. The centre stone is missing – so too is the plank linking the gap, which requires a six-foot jump from one stone to another!

Hathersage is an interesting village, nesting below high moorland. Charlotte Brontë stayed here and was inspired to write Jane Eyre, the 'Eyre' perpetuating the name of an ancient local family, and substituting the name 'Morton' for Hathersage. More interestingly, Hathersage was said to be the home of John Little, who became Robin Hood's chief companion 'Little John', and his grave is to be found in Hathersage churchyard. The church itself is one of my favourites; it is beautifully lit with attractive stained-glass windows, and has a calm, relaxing atmosphere.

On the higher (Sheffield) road the views of the valley are simply superb. One particular corner is known as 'Surprise View'; as visitors coming towards Hathersage from the moors suddenly encounter the breath-taking spectacle of the Derwent Valley. Beyond, in an area of ancient human settlements are the brooding hill forts of Carl's Wark and Higgar Tor.

Along the valley floor, the Derwent winds its way past the village, and the location we see in the painting is at Leadmill Bridge a mile downstream. I had intended to paint the bridge itself, but this beautiful glade next to the River inspired me with its beech trees in their full Autumn glory. I sketched the scene with charcoal, to paint afterwards as a watercolour, whilst my family enjoyed a picnic. We had come to the end of a short walking holiday which included a treck over Kinder Scout, Back Tor and Lose Hill, then on this particular day from Bradwell, Abney and Abney Clough to Leadmill Bridge, so those who know the area can appreciate that we enjoyed a well-earned rest.

Stepping Stones at Hathersage

Footbridge at Bamford Mill

10. COPPICE WOOD

The path from Leadmill bridge to Grindleford a couple of miles downstream passes through a small woodland known as Coppice Wood on the east side of the River. This is a delightful place to visit in Spring, and I have tried to capture the fresh seasonal atmosphere in the painting. What I wasn't able to include was the bird song, which is such a feature of this woodland as it seems to echo from the high leafy canopy. Many of our common warblers are seen here, especially the chiff-chaff and the willow warbler, but you may be lucky enough to see their more unusual cousin, the wood warbler.

This stretch of the Derwent is the most likely place to see a goosander, an unusual duck which has undergone a population explosion in the last decade. Most bird books will tell you it is restricted to Scotland, but its journey south has been rapid, through Cumbria, Northumberland, Yorkshire and now Derbyshire. It finds the middle reaches of the Derwent ideal and is flourishing here, but has been seen on the River as far south as Derby. Accompanied by up to 10 young ducklings in early May, its feeding technique is to swim upstream in the shallows tapping the stones with its bill, dashing suddenly to catch a disturbed fish. The small fluffy young copy the adults but take insects as well as small fry. The goosander's love of fish has long caused it to be persecuted, but it seems to be safe on the Derwent where I imagine its diet consists largely of bullheads, loaches, eels and minnows, with the occasional trout or grayling from deeper water.

Coppice Wood is located in an area surrounded by splendid countryside. Whilst this statement could apply to much of Derbyshire this is one of the most beautiful areas of the Longshaw Estate – now owned by the National Trust. It offers great scenery and fascinating walks along woodland paths, streams and moorland where there is evidence of Iron Age settlements.

A walk along Padley Gorge comes highly recommended, the path along this valley following Burbage Brook as it tumbles downwards to the Derwent, its passage marked by rock pools and waterfalls. There is a designated nature trail with much to see and enjoy in this ancient woodland, and if you did not spot a wood warbler in Coppice Wood you will definitely see one here. They are easily distinguished from the chiff-chaff and willow warbler by their larger size, brighter yellow-green colouring, and richer song.

For a mid-morning snack I can also recommend the café at Grindleford station which serves strong tea in pint mugs and thick, calorific fruit cake designed to keep you going for at least ten miles. Padley Chapel, built in the fifteenth century has been restored, and an annual pilgrimage on the Thursday nearest to July 20 honours the memory of the priests who were taken from here to Derby for a martyr's death in 1588.

This area is beautiful throughout the whole year, but like any woodland it is at its best in Spring and Autumn. If you visit in the Summer, a word of warning – be careful where you sit especially in Coppice Wood. You may find you are sharing your beautiful surroundings with thousands of wood ants.

Burbage Brook in Padley Gorge

11. FROM CURBAR EDGE

There are many high points from which you can enjoy magnificent panoramic views over the Derwent Valley. The upper reaches of the River offer superb views; so do the slopes around the reservoirs, the precipitous gorge between Matlock and Cromford and the gentler wooded slopes around Ambergate to name a few, but one of the best must surely be the gritstone edges between Baslow and Froggatt. There is a car park on Curbar Edge that offers easy access.

The stone faces of the edge are up to 40 feet high and composed of huge solid blocks of gritstone with deep horizontal and vertical fissures; the rock offers a firm grip even in the wet and is not prone to flaking or splintering. It therefore provides an ideal rock-climbing venue, and its easy climbs make it eminently suitable for beginners. This is a sport that requires proper instruction, and teaching sessions are frequently in progress here. There are even some climbs along Curbar and Froggatt Edges to tax the teachers. I was surprised to find that guidebooks are available showing climbers every minute detail of each rock face worthy of a climb.

Derbyshire gritstone, a coarse hard sandstone, has always been prized as an excellent material for millstones; in fact it is known as millstone grit. If you look below the edge you see numerous examples of millstones – no doubt ones which broke or were faulty in some way. It is surprising how far they were sent; I recently visited a water mill in Kent and was told by the curator that Derbyshire millstones had always been used there. It must have been a huge journey whether by wheeled transport or by boat in the eighteenth century with something so heavy but clearly the properties of this stone made it worthwhile.

The stones were roughly prepared at the rock face and carefully rolled down the hillside to a waiting wagon. This movement was facilitated by threading an axle through the millstone's centre, then with a few heavy lads on either side the stone was cautiously wheeled down. I'm sure there must have been more than one occasion when the millstone took control, gathered speed and went careering down the hillside hell bent on destroying the village of Curbar. 'Take cover – here comes another!'

My first experience of Curbar Edge goes back to the tender age of ten, when as a primary school child we stayed at Longshaw Lodge for a school holiday. The head teacher was an enthusiastic walker and took us for long rambles, which probably awakened my interest in hiking. On one of these walks on Curbar Edge the heavens opened and the whole class was soaked to the skin. I have never walked along here without thinking about that drenching!

The last occasion, and the one on which I prepared this painting, reversed the situation. A torrential downpour had just stopped so I slipped from the shelter of the car to encounter this lovely image as the sun started to emerge over the Derwent valley. In the distance we can just see the River where it forms a wide stretch below the New Bridge. The River's course is marked with trees, mostly alders, which clothe its banks for much of its journey (and have often obstructed some splendid views).

Abandoned millstone

12. NEW BRIDGE

About half a mile north of Calver village a weir across the Derwent creates a lake-like stretch of water, at the northern end of which is New Bridge. The eastern bank from which you should have the best views is very overgrown with willow and alder but there are one or two places where you can squeeze through to see this view in my painting. In the late Spring the area is carpeted with wild garlic, a common plant throughout this middle range of the River, whilst Indian Balsam forges through the undergrowth to provide a show of rose-pink flowers in the Summer.

The weir and the start of the mill stream are some distance upstream from the mill, presumably to generate a sufficient head of water. The mill itself is an imposing structure and is being converted into flats and apartments. The new occupants will enjoy unrivalled views – no doubt reflected in the prices – down on to the Derwent and up to Curbar Edge.

West of New Bridge, we come to the delightful villages of Stoney Middleton and Eyam, this last village experiencing one of the most devastating events in the county's history. Outbreaks of bubonic plague had always occurred from time to time, but normally in cities, and the incidence in remote villages like Eyam was unusual. The story of its occurrence in Eyam draws thousands of people to this 'Plague' village.

In 1665 when the plague struck the first few cases were not immediately recognised but the horror soon dawned. Those who had somewhere to go quickly fled, but one of the cornerstones of the Eyam story was that the village introduced a system of isolation and containment to prevent the spread of the disease to the neighbouring villages. The new Rector, the Rev W. Mompesson is credited with this action and worked tirelessly to help the sick. Surrounding villages were naturally on 'red alert' and the story is told of a carter who was apprehended after it was known that he had passed through the village and was examined by a doctor who was on the other side of the Derwent!

After Eyam's food supplies dwindled they received supplies from outside; food being left at outlying locations and money in payment placed in vinegar – trusting to its powers as a disinfectant.

The plague reputedly reached Eyam from London (where it was raging) in a chest of cloth and clothing patterns and the first victim was the travelling tailor who had arranged its delivery.

The pace of death soon increased and spread through the village like wildfire, abating in the winter and returning the next year. Its progress is charted in a book of remembrance in the church where the names and dates of death of those who succumbed are poignantly recorded. Out of a population of 350 only 83 survived. It must have been a truly horrific experience. Any day you could expect a member of your family, a life-long friend or you yourself to exhibit the first dreaded signs and await an unpleasant death.

Calver Mill

Ashley Bryant

13. HIGH SUMMER AT BASLOW

This view shows the corn-mill, weir and lovely old bridge in the distance. Having completed this watercolour I noticed a few weeks later an almost identical view in Hope-Moncrieff's book on *Derbyshire* published in 1927 and it is interesting to note that the scene has remained unchanged. Baslow offers many interesting opportunities for the artist, especially around Bridge End, the oldest part of the village.

The bridge was built at the very end of the Tudor period replacing an even earlier wooden toll bridge. In those days six shillings and eight pence (33p) was levied for carting a pair of millstones across but there was probably no easy alternative to this exorbitant charge. The new stone bridge continued the practice of charging tolls; the strange 'cage' seen in its walls was actually a toll-keeper's shelter. The bridge now finds itself in a quiet backwater of a busy village, the large volume of traffic passing over the Devonshire bridge downstream.

Baslow is an active centre – active in the sense that it attracts a lot of tourists as the 'gateway' to Chatsworth but also in the fact that there are flourishing local interests and societies. It is undoubtedly a commuter village for Sheffield, but in my experience it is often the newcomers who get involved, join committees and bring in ideas, enthusiasm and 'new blood' to a community.

The custom of well-dressing is virtually unique to Derbyshire and can be seen in Baslow and many other villages throughout Spring and Summer. With its origins rooted in pagan times it was a ceremony that paid tribute to a source of water, or water spirits or gods. A water supply was naturally important, if not the most important consideration in siting a settlement – a feature difficult to appreciate now when cold comes out of one tap and hot out of the other. It is thought that the Black Death in the fourteenth century re-affirmed the practice but the present ceremony, very much a Christian one, provides a service of thanksgiving and blesses the well, which is adorned with a tableau of outstanding design and workmanship in petals and natural materials.

The process starts by covering a panel with a layer of wet clay, on which a carefully worked-out design is meticulously inscribed. This is blocked-in with a variety of materials – mostly flower petals, but also leaves, seeds and berries to create a magnificent but temporary work of art. The detailed care and attention has to be seen to be believed. For example, I watched in amazement as thousands of blue hydrangea petals were laid out on a table and graded from marginally darker to lighter shades so they could be selected to create subtle changes of tone and colour across an area of background. Small seeds in their hundreds were applied with fine tweezers and for my contribution I was allowed to place one in position!

In recent years well dressings have increased even further in popularity and are being re-introduced or are starting in places where they never existed. It is an activity for all ages and members of each community and has been known to generate healthy rivalry!

Preparing for the Well dressings

14. CHATSWORTH

When reviewing possible locations for paintings of the Derwent at the outset of my project there were several views that I considered essential. The start and the beginning of the River were important, and then came a flurry of other essential views, including Chatsworth.

As a child I recall car journeys through Chatsworth Park and adults saying 'Look at the deer, Ashley'. I could never see them as they were always in the distance. Amusingly, this moved on a generation; when I drove through the park with my own children they never saw the deer I pointed out to them. The deer, therefore, became an important ingredient in my painting of Chatsworth.

Here, by the Derwent, is undoubtedly one of the greatest stately homes of Britain. I recall a recent visit to the Cotswolds where I met a German couple who seem to have visited every stately home and every National Trust and English Heritage property in Britain. 'Go to Chatsworth,' they marvelled. 'It's the best place we have ever been to!'

I cannot possibly do justice to the many wonders of Chatsworth in these few paragraphs, but there are two small features in particular that never fail to impress me. Like all visitors I am amazed at the realism of the violin painted on the back of the door in the State Music Room. This trompe l'oeil by Jan van der Vaart is so real that no one believes it can possibly be painted on a flat surface. Having tried wood-carving and achieved some reasonable results myself, I am in awe of Grindling Gibbons magnificent lime-wood carving of a lace cravat, woodcock and dead leaves displayed on the Oak Stairs. Its details astound me.

The Old Mill in Chatsworth Park

The Painted Hall is one of Chatworth's many wonders; the upper walls and ceiling show the original paintings by Laguerre depicting the life of Caesar, the ceiling fortunately saved from collapsing in the 1930s. The State rooms are Chatsworth's grandest, and were designed principally for show, to house the First Duke's many treasures and to provide more-than-adequate quarters if royalty dropped in, which did not happen until Queen Victoria paid a visit. The State Dining Room is sumptuous and completely original with a painted ceiling by the celebrated Verrio. Amusingly, in one classical painting he incorporated a portrait of the First Duke's housekeeper whom he disliked, 'cutting the thread of life'.

The treasures of Chatsworth seem to be endless and the paintings, sculptures, porcelain and furniture are the finest you will see anywhere, but they are not all in the traditional and classical mould. It is interesting to see the changes in the approach to portraiture as we look at the Devonshires depicted over many generations in The Sketch Galleries. The stuffy portraits of Victorian times make way to those of the twentieth century revealing much more personality and vitality. Chatsworth continues to collect art treasures and purchases works by contemporary artists, even some which may be considered avant-garde such as Lucian Freud's 'Large Interior'.

In these brief notes I can do little justice to Chatsworth's many treasures and I have not mentioned the gardens and parkland! As an artist I could spend weeks in this place gaining inspiration and ideas.

15. BRIGHT WINTER'S MORNING

I have mentioned that some locations on the Derwent were on my 'essential' list of subjects to paint but there have been many attractive locations that I have found simply by walking the riverbank. This is one of those 'in the middle of nowhere' examples that I came across one January morning on the footpath southwards from Chatsworth Park. The location is about a mile north of Rowsley.

One of the most important aspects of any landscape is the quality of the light, and interesting and atmospheric lighting can transform even the most uninspiring of subjects. Most people taking up art as a hobby become more observant; they start to notice the changing light on the landscape, the characteristics of shadows, the drama achieved by light, and ultimately the way they can use light to advantage in their own paintings. However, it is always easier to see than to imagine, and this particular view of the Derwent came 'ready-made' with a sparkling, bright, crisp Winter's morning.

People often ask if I paint my Winter scenes direct from the landscape. The answer is not usually; in fact all the main paintings in this book have been produced from sketches and photographs. Most paintings have taken a few days to complete, and it is not practical to sit on the spot for this length of time whilst the weather and the lighting conditions change!

Working from photographs does not mean that I simply copy them to produce a painting. Far from it, the photographs I take are simply used as pieces of information and provide a quick method of establishing topographical accuracy. From these and my sketches, I sometimes adjust the viewpoint, change the lighting or atmospheric conditions, the colours, the time of day or even the season of the year. Items can be omitted, simplified or added. Before I start on a painting I conjure up a vision of the finished result and each brush-stroke works towards this goal. I always tell my students they should never paint in 'hope'; the interpretation of their landscapes has to be conceived, assessed, developed and finalised before the first brush-stroke is applied.

I love to sketch 'on the spot' and most of the charcoal drawings in this book are produced in this way. Charcoal is a wonderful medium for working quickly and loosely, and one of its major advantages is that half-tones – the various shades of grey – can be achieved quickly. In fact your second finger does most of the work by smudging the lines into soft shapes. Sharp detail is difficult to achieve at first, but a stick of charcoal wears quickly into an edge or point. This can be used to create fine detail for a few strokes until it wears down, then re-sharpened again by hatching across an area of shading. In this way you move back and forth between different areas of the drawing – an odd technique but you get used to it.

I do paint on-the-spot occasionally, and I vividly recall an outing to Allestree Lake one very cold Winter's day. I set up my easel and commenced an oil painting. The wind-sprang up, but not to be deterred I applied guy ropes to the easel. It was so cold the oil paints were almost freezing and I had to 'walk on the spot' as I painted to keep warm. Finally, a large gust of wind blew my easel over and the canvas flew through the air to land the wrong way down on dusty earth, pine needles and old leaves!

Riverside meadows near Rowsley

Ashley Bryant

16. DARLEY BRIDGE

The Derwent is not the clearest of rivers. Rising as it does on peaty moorland the water is stained a brown or orange – the colour of a good malt whisky!

After receiving the clear waters of the Wye two miles upstream the Derwent is given a Spring clean, and this view from Darley Bridge looks more like a southern chalk stream. Long streamers of bright weed trail across beds of sand and gravel and in the gaps trout rise to flies.

On the downstream side of the bridge an alternative view unfolds. The ancient bridge of five arches is reflected in a smooth, calm surface which soon breaks into ripples over a stony bed. Children often paddle here and attempt to collect small fry in their fishing nets, and the banks are full with comfrey and buttercups. A small parking area completes the list of everything you require for a painting expedition.

This, of course, is during the Summer months. I have seen the bridge with water almost to the tops of the arches, lakes of flood water across the landscape, the pub near the bridge awash and the small village of Darley Bridge sand-bagged and distinctly uncomfortable.

Darley Dale is largely a ribbon development along the A6, a slow bumper-to-bumper journey most weekends. One of Darley's most influential residents – Sir Joseph Whitworth – developed a standard screw thread in the nineteenth century, which made him a fortune. He left a legacy of the Whitworth Hospital, Institute and Park and the two miles of stone-walling of all properties fronting the A6. This oddity keeps me mildly amused and that traffic never seems so bad!

For the art-minded I can recommend a visit to St Helen's church to see a lovely stained-glass window by the Pre-Raphaelite artist, Edward Burne-Jones, which enhances this mainly fourteenth century church. A yew tree in the church-yard is reputed to be one of Britain's biggest and oldest. Continuing along the road to Darley Dale Station we find Peak Rail, where steam trains provide another interesting feature and the subject of my next painting.

Over the western side of the valley Stanton Moor reveals a treasure of great antiquity – a stone circle. Visiting this one Summer's evening was a great spiritual experience – the moor of heather and woodland suddenly opened out into a wide clearing to reveal the stone circle – the Nine Ladies. It is not perfectly circular, and the spacing of stones is uniform in parts and not in others. Who made it, why and when are questions we shall never answer, but the mystery only adds to its power. We left well after 10pm, the evening still warm, and wonderfully atmospheric. Woodcock were flying overhead with their strange 'roding' displays, otherwise there was complete quiet and calm as my son and I returned in the gathering twilight.

There are continuing attempts to open quarries on the edge of the moor and I trust this will never happen to this sacred place. My support is with those who oppose such developments, who cherish this natural beauty and act as guardians against its desecration.

Fun for all Darley Bridge

Ashley Bryant

17. THE FLYING SCOTSMAN

In the 1960s as steam power on Britain's railways drew to a close and massive investment was required to update the rail system the favoured form of transport switched to roads. Railway lines were closed in the Beeching and post-Beeching eras, and emphasis was placed on motorways so that Dagenham and Longbridge reigned supreme. It was in this climate that the main railway line from Derby to Manchester was severed between Matlock and Buxton in 1968, an act seen even without hindsight as one of sheer folly.

In the 1970s a group of enthusiasts formed a society to restore the line. This 'impossible dream' as it was known, has at least been partly realised and the line has been restored for about four miles from a halt just north of Matlock's station to a new station of Rowsley South. This route along the Derwent Valley is undoubtedly the easiest segment of the near 20-mile stretch to Buxton, the remainder requiring expenditure way beyond Peak Rail's resources. Recently, however, Railtrack have expressed interest in re-opening the line and are conducting detailed surveys in conjunction with Derbyshire County Council. This route should ease road congestion if a well-organised park-and-ride system is introduced, but would this allow even more people in the Peak District? I am sure that whatever scheme is adopted the motorist will continue to take up the slack.

At present steam trains ply up and down the restored section of line where Peak Rail operate their heritage railway. A visit by the world's most famous steam locomotive, 'The Flying Scotsman', in August 2000 enabled me to paint this watercolour. This particular locomotive had recently been purchased, and restored at enormous expense by a Derbyshire-born businessman, who may base this engine at his 'steam fair' at Ambergate, a few miles south.

The River is not in evidence but is immediately to the right of the scene as we look south to Matlock, and Riber Castle can just be seen on the hillside.

A flourishing tram museum attracts crowds of enthusiasts at Crich, several miles south-east of here, and at Butterley the Midland Railway Centre provides yet more exciting times for the steam railway enthusiast.

Near Peak Rail's terminus

18. THE RAFT RACE

This amazing event for participants and spectators alike is held on Boxing Day along a course from Matlock to Cromford, around two miles. This race has inspired many others since its origin in the early 1960s, when two energetic members of a local scuba diving club decided they would liven up Boxing Day with a race along the Derwent. They each jumped on quickly assembled collections of tyre inner tubes and raced each other, the incident ignited widespread interest and the next year they were joined by others. The rest, as they say, is history.

The event is organised by the Derbyshire Association of Sub Aqua Clubs, and the original impetus to the growth of the event stemmed from the challenges between the Matlock Diving Club and other sub aqua clubs. The event is still essentially for members of diving clubs, since there is a clear need to be a good swimmer, to be able to experience mishaps without panic and to have wet suits and proper clothing. However, many more people slip into the event with 'unauthorised' craft.

The route along a very turbulent stretch of the Derwent starts at the car park upstream of Matlock Bridge and finishes, for those who make it, at Cromford Meadows. There are numerous hazards, the first being Matlock Bridge itself, a collision sends rafts and their occupants spinning into the choppy waters, followed by the bends and rapids after Hall Leys Gardens and the rapids at the canoe slalom course at High Tor, but the weir and rough water at Masson Mill prove to be the undoing of those who think the end is in sight.

The number of rafts in the event varies but there are normally up to two hundred craft of all descriptions, some plain and functional, some appearing well designed (who can really tell?), whilst others are flamboyant, highly decorated and have taken a huge amount of effort. Many of course, are untested and have never been floated on water until the moment of launch. That 'sinking feeling' is not unknown; when all hands climb aboard, some rafts fall apart whilst others do not wish to be steered in any direction other than directly into the piers of Matlock Bridge!

Three hundred yards from the start of the race the first batch of casualties emerges, as competitors are seen hanging on to fragments of rafts or standing bewildered in the churning waters of the Derwent, senses numbed by water as cold as it gets before freezing. 'It takes a few years to develop the ideal raft' remarked one participant. 'It's a case of the right balance between sturdiness and flexibility'. I conceded I would need to make no such compromises as a spectator and regretted that I could only be in one place at a time to see the event.

The spectacle draws huge crowds, and what better way of spending a couple of hours on Boxing Day? Although Matlock is as far from the sea as possible in the British Isles it is appropriate that the beneficiary of donations and sponsorship monies raised by the event is the Royal National Lifeboat Institution.

Inevitable casualties

19. MATLOCK GORGE

For several miles the Derwent has had an easy time, flowing through gently sloping valleys and even meandering over a flood plain on its way to Matlock, but suddenly it encounters a dramatic barrier – a towering limestone hill up to eleven hundred feet high and two miles long. This provides some of the most spectacular scenery in Britain and I make no apologies for including quite a number of paintings of this location. I recently brought an artist friend to the area from Essex, who declared it was simply unfair to have all this inspirational scenery in such a concentrated area!

The painting opposite shows the Derwent as it leaves Hall Leys Gardens at Matlock and is deflected when it encounters the towering limestone. Over past epochs the River has obviously found its way through the limestone, widening and wearing away cracks and fissures until it carved out the dramatic gorge we see today. The eastern side rises vertically in places, and the rock faces show signs of erosion from the River. The western slopes are less steep although 'very steep' is a term you would use if you tried to walk up Masson Hill to the Heights of Abraham – named in the mid eighteenth century to reflect General Wolfe's death at the place of the same name in Canada. From the A6 below it is a fair climb and my wife will always point up to the top and say to friends 'he made me walk up there when we were first married'. Nowadays the cable car takes the strain.

At the summit there are two caverns which were worked for lead from Roman times, and these, the Rutland and Masson Caverns are open to the public. The views and walks on this hill are superb. To the south through a clearing in the trees we can see Matlock Bath way down below, and opposite over the steep slopes of the gorge and High Tor to Riber Castle perched 800 feet over Matlock.

This mock castle, which is such a prominent landmark of the area, was built in the mid nineteenth century by John Smedley, a hosiery manufacturer, as his own residence. It is a giant, blackened gritstone structure, already eroded by the perpetual winds that blow there, unoccupied and deemed to be unsafe, although part of the castle grounds have been used as a wildlife reserve for years.

Smedley's name is associated with his 'Hydro', the large building on Matlock Bank he constructed as a spa where people could take the restorative waters. He seems to have imposed a tough regime on his clients, with a largely vegetarian diet, cold showers, meditation, no alcohol or tobacco and adherence to a strict timetable. I'm sure his wealthy customers who indulged in the excesses of the day came out leaner, fitter and healthier, and unquestionably Smedley's Victorian version of the modern 'health farm' brought him great success.

Across High Tor to Riber Castle

20. RIVERSIDE WALK IN SUMMER

The choice of painting for Matlock Bath proved to be difficult since there are so many subjects to choose in this amazing place. This 'inland seaside resort' is as far from the sea as possible, and is squeezed into the limestone gorge where it forms a one-street township. In true seaside style it has an amusement arcade, souvenir shops, tea rooms, cafes and a promenade along the Derwent with its seaside sounding 'North and South Parades.' Bed and breakfast places are thick on the ground and Gulliver's Kingdom entertains the kids. Who needs the sea anyway.

As the name suggests Matlock Bath like Matlock itself was a spa town where people came to take the curative waters. On the steep hillside to the west are early nineteenth century villas, many built by the wealthy who came here to ease their ailments.

I have brought many people to Derbyshire over the years, and impressive as the county is – even spectacular in parts – there is nothing that astonishes the visitor more than Matlock Bath. I watch their faces peering out of the car windows as I drive through and listen to their 'wow'-type comments. It's not too difficult to divert my eyes from the road to watch their reactions, as most people familiar with the A6 will know that the traffic here is frequently and seriously gridlocked.

I have lived away from Derbyshire for over thirty years and the biggest changes I notice are the dreadful traffic jams especially on the A6. However, in Matlock Bath the traffic has always been slow moving and only the smallest changes have occurred since I was a boy. But what's happening on the promenade! New buildings are being erected with a sign proclaiming 'Victorian-style shopping development'! Originally there were buildings on the riverside of the road but these were demolished when the road was widened. And so this new development brings us back full circle.

Like many seaside resorts Matlock Bath indulges in 'illuminations', that old seaside practice of prolonging the tourist season. As a child I remember being dragged off to Blackpool on cold October weekends to 'see the lights' from freezing open-topped trams. Do people do that anymore? You bet – they come to Matlock Bath in their thousands, stroll along the Lover's walks and love every minute of it. Venetian nights and firework displays provide the icing on the cake. I must confess a secret liking for the place myself but then I love old seaside towns with their faded glory.

Gulliver's Kingdom is a place to take the kids and I can vouch for its effectiveness. Model villages, fun fares, ghost train, assault course and picnic centres in the forest provide something for most children from two to seventy-five. A day spent here burns off a lot of energy.

At the north end of Matlock Bath you can take a cable car ride to the Heights of Abraham or watch the canoeists on the slalom course as the Derwent races over its solid rock bed in the limestone gorge. High above on High Tor almost 400 feet above the River the sheer smooth rock face of carboniferous limestone presents one of the most difficult of climbs, tackled only by experts, and you can watch for hours as they scale upwards inch by inch. Visitors to High Tor grounds can be seen near the edge of the precipice as they admire the views, and as a person who doesn't like heights – at least these sorts of heights, I find this alarming.

One very obvious alternative to all this activity is to take a leisurely stroll along the promenade, have the occasional ice cream or a fish and chip tea, then bask in the proximity of many other people enjoying themselves in the same way!

When it came to a painting all this variety left me spoilt for choice. It was tempting to produce a whole exhibition – full of Matlock Bath scenes. Finally however, I decided to paint the calm side of the Derwent, away from the main stream of humanity. Here, little groups of people stroll along the riverside path opposite the Pavilion and enjoy a glorious Summer's afternoon. On this eastern side of the Derwent paths also wind up the limestone cliffs high above the River affording superb views of the town and over to Masson Hill on the west bank. Matlock Bath certainly provides a lot for all ages and all energy levels.

Ashley Bryant

21. RIVERSIDE WALK IN WINTER

An out-of-season stop in Matlock is to be recommended; it is easier to park and you have relative calmness and space. Don't expect to have the place to yourself though since a little ray of sunshine will still bring out the tourists.

There are some interesting shops along the 'Front' and in the arcades, where you can find antiques, paintings, pottery and new-age outlets with everything from crystals to clothing. However, Winter offers a good opportunity for a little walking around the area, and at this time of the year the lack of foliage on the trees opens up the views, which are spectacular as you ascend the valley. The hills are pretty steep though, but at least in the Winter you do not overheat!

You can walk along the east bank of the Derwent from Matlock to Matlock Bath for most of the way, which offers a pleasant flat walk, but if you possess an excess of energy and you don't mind heights the path over High Tor provides breath-taking views, before you descend through mature woodland to the cable car station at Matlock Bath.

The cable car takes you across the Derwent up the west side of the valley, and over a steeply wooded hillside, pausing briefly half way for you to enjoy the panorama, then continuing to its summit at the Heights of Abraham. For those who want to go even higher a tower with a spiral staircase leads to a viewing platform from which you can see that the earth is truly round. The hillsides abound with footpaths and an excellent leaflet on walking in the area is available from Tourist Information.

The Mining Museum housed in the Victoria Pavilion is just the place to visit on a cold day. Derbyshire's history is tied very closely to mining and the county has provided a major source of lead from Roman times, but many types of minerals have been extracted including the semi-precious stone, Blue John.

Except for the worst weather Matlock Bath is a mecca for motorcyclists. Each weekend hundreds of them congregate along the 'Front' to swap stories, admire each other's machines and have a good day out. Gone are the BSA Rocket Gold Stars, Norton Dominators, Triumphs and Vincents of my teenage years, replaced by Kawasakis, Yamahas and Ducatis so stylish that they look as though they are travelling at a hundred miles an hour when they are stationary. Occasionally someone arrives on a 'classic' bike, which creates a great deal of attention. The average age of the owners has changed; those enthusiasts now look older than they did in the early 1960s. Being an old rocker myself I'm tempted to borrow my son's moped and join them one Sunday.

The riverside path on the east bank forms the subject of my second painting of Matlock Bath. This softly lit, calm, cold, frosty morning inspired me to paint the scene; the occasion was unusual as there was no one around on this lovely tranquil walk. White is a colour that is used cautiously in watercolour painting, and for areas of white such as snow or frost the white of the paper is used. It means you have to be rather careful where you apply the paint. The small painting on this page shows an Autumn view across the River over to Masson Hill.

Autumn Tints at Matlock Bath

Ashley Bryant

22. MASSON MILL

After our sojourn in Matlock Bath we approach the end of the limestone gorge on our route south, and discover a new chapter in the River's story.

From here to Derby, cotton mills were constructed in the eighteenth century, which brought employment to the region and great prosperity to their owners. These mills harnessed water power to drive the new technology of spinning cotton and effectively nurtured and developed the early stages of the industrial revolution. The mills of Masson, Cromford, Belper, Milford, Peckwash (Duffield), Darley Abbey and Derby are now receiving increasing recognition for their historic contribution, so much so that World Heritage Status has been proposed for this corridor of the Derwent. This accolade could bring in many more visitors to the region.

The introduction of raw cotton from America in the eighteenth century, provided a new material that was lightweight, hard wearing, washable, comfortable and naturally white, but easily dyed. These properties made it ideal for clothing which had hitherto been made principally of linen or wool. All that was needed was a method of automating the production of threads, and manufacturing garments – a tall order, but ingenious minds were working on it.

Richard Arkwright arrived on the scene at a timely moment. Born in Preston he was a barber and wigmaker until he was middle-aged, but his skills lay in engineering and his interests in cotton spinning. Concerned with the Luddite presence in Lancashire he moved to Nottingham to continue his developments in spinning machinery, and set up a cotton mill using horse-power. Here, he met Jedediah Strutt about whom we will hear later, and their partnership proved fruitful. It was Strutt who helped to finance Arkwright's enterprise when the banks proved to be over cautious, and he also helped with some fine-tuning of equipment.

Arkwright had developed an automated spinning machine which he was now perfecting; this equipment teased out the cotton fibres into a uniform volume and flow then spun them into a thread. Connected to a source of water power this could drive up to 24 spinning heads, and each operator ultimately controlled two machines giving a huge increase in productivity. This machine, when driven by water, was termed the 'water frame', and as Arkwright's key invention it helped to make his fortune.

In seeking water power Arkwright found a suitable location at Cromford, a remote Derbyshire village at that time, where the Derwent surges through the end of the limestone gorge. An ideal location in some respects – at least there was water power in reserve – but it was not simply a case of building a mill with a 'Job Vacancies' sign in the window. The area was underpopulated and road access was almost impossible.

Inducements were made to operators, and houses were constructed in the village of Cromford, attracting a labour force. In fact Arkwright practically built a worker village with communal facilities, and Cromford with its solid housing is sought after today, being an attractive stone-built village just off the busy A6.

Masson Mill was Arkwright's second location at Cromford and was built in 1783 a few hundred yards upstream from his original Cromford Mill. At Masson Mill he used a conventional system for tapping off the River water by building a weir and a sluice, which has the advantages that water of constant power can be shut off or diverted if necessary. Access to this mill was a problem and eventually the end of the gorge had to be blasted away to form a narrow road – always a bottleneck to traffic until it was widened in the 1960s.

In its wooded limestone gorge the mill offers and unrivalled setting. My painting of Masson Mill views the River, mill stream and mill on a cold Winter's night. I had considered an Autumn scene with soft hazy light, but like many of the artists at the time the mill was constructed I was drawn to the idea of a moonlit scene, where the reflections of light sparkle on the waters. Can you imagine working a long shift here on a night like this, with inadequate lighting and no heating? The industrial age had arrived!

Masson Mill has been developed into a visitor centre with the usual range of tourist shops, and a car park has been tacked on the end of the southern range of mill buildings.

Ashley Bryant

23. SUMMER DOWNPOUR

I sketched this scene on the worst day of Summer; a tropical downpour created a mist over the River and the leaves hung heavy on the trees. The side of Masson Mill peeps into the far left to locate the scene and the small picture on this page looks downstream from this same point.

As we move downstream further we come to Arkwright's first mill at Cromford. Built in 1771, this was the first water-powered cotton spinning mill in the world, and it has great historical significance. Oddly enough his mill did not use water power from the River unlike the later Masson Mill, but from the Bonsall Brook and a drain from lead workings (known locally as a sough) which were taken by aqueduct to the mill. This must have been sufficient, and indeed water was also used from here to supply the Cromford Canal for some years until the Leawood Pumping Station was built.

Any business needs to maximise the use of capital and Arkwright's mills operated twenty-four hours a day. Candle-lit at night they attracted tourists to marvel at the spectacle. Amongst the visitors were many artists, the most notable of whom was Joseph Wright of Derby, who was later commissioned to paint the rotund and successful Sir Richard, proudly holding a model of his water frame.

It is interesting to conjecture about life and working conditions in these mills – no doubt it was very hard, and the hours were over-long. If you were not up to scratch you could easily be replaced; you were not paid if you were sick and would often need to work if you felt ill. Any misdemeanour would lose you not only your job but your house. The work force was kept strictly in control but there is no reason to think that Arkwright was any different from other employers of his day.

Arkwright's fame brought him great fortune and it is said one year he gave each of his ten children £10,000 at Christmas. Not bad for a one-time barber! He also built himself the 'palace' of Willersley Castle on the eastern side of the Derwent valley overlooking his mills. This building, mill-like in design, caught fire during construction, delaying progress. However, no-one can cheat death, a great man no more than any of us, and Arkwright never saw it completed. In his lifetime he is reputed to have planted 100,000 trees around the area and it is certainly a leafy valley.

Today there is a flourishing Arkwright Society, which continues to promote his achievements and to research aspects of his work.

Cromford Mill now houses a visitor centre, offering tours. Here we see the original designs of the Mill and the place where he developed and nurtured his business practices, a 'model' that was copied throughout Britain, stimulating the industrial revolution. There are also some craft workshops and bookshops and a tea-room, but I feel that far more restoration should be carried out to the fabric of these old buildings, and there is still much work to be done to make a first-class tourist attraction.

24. FROM CROMFORD BRIDGE

The Derwent finally escapes from its limestone walls at Cromford and creates a wide expanse of level flood-plain known as Cromford Meadows. This painting looks down on the River from the fifteenth century bridge situated a short distance downstream from Arkwright's original mill, and the wharf and terminus of the Cromford Canal.

The season is mid-Autumn and the River is still shallow and clear, but a month from now when the leaves have fallen from the trees and the water surges along after heavy rains it will present quite a different picture.

Cromford Meadows provide an ideal venue for carnivals and fêtes and the flat ground is home to a number of sports pitches – it is quite a number of years since I played rugby here for my school against a local Matlock School.

Cromford Bridge is something of an oddity; it was clearly widened a long time ago, there are pointed arches on the downstream side and curved arches on the other. No doubt the person widening the bridge had a good reason for changing it, but this has long been forgotten.

This bridge claims some fame in having a bridge chapel attached to it, although this is derelict. As we can see from the little painting its restoration is beyond consideration since only half the walls survive. Sited just a few yards away is an eighteenth century fishing temple, the inscription over its entrance 'Piscatoribus Sacrum' testifying to the Derwent's reputation as an excellent fishing river in the days when salmon were common-place. Izaak Walton, the great exponent in the art of fishing, and the author of the *Compleat Angler*, visited Derbyshire for fishing expeditions. He fished the River Dove, but it is highly likely he also tried his skills on the Derwent.

This location is easy to reach and there is a vast area of car parking space on the Meadows. It s a lovely place to sit on a Summer's evening to watch trout rising in the River and even the possibility of seeing a kingfisher as it flashes along the Derwent. Little grebes dabble and dive in the calmer water near the far bank and these entertaining birds are even more common on the canal nearby.

25. BY CROMFORD MEADOWS

This was one of my first paintings for this series on the Derwent and I remember climbing up and down the bank here on a wet Summer's day to find a suitable viewpoint. I distinctly remember slipping down on the wet vegetation to land on my backside in the River! Since that day three years ago there have been a few similar occasions – it's like being a child again.

This particular stretch of River sweeps around Comford Meadows just downstream of the railway bridge and provides fast flowing shallows on the near side with a deeper channel on the far side. The Derwent – and this is a typical stretch – is one of the best in the country for grayling, a silvery fish related to trout and distinguished easily by its extra large dorsal fin. It uses this rather like a spoiler to hold itself in strong currents. Like all the trout family it needs clean, well-oxygenated water, and appears to be extending its range further downstream in the River.

It was here on my first painting expedition that I saw my very first goosander – a drake, which raced downstream swimming at great speed in the strong current. I could hardly believe my eyes but they have become familiar to me since. At this spot on a late Spring visit I was delighted to see a family of goosanders – a duck and eight ducklings, and I rapidly produced this charcoal sketch.

Dippers are common on the Derwent but the numbers decline as we move south. They like fast-flowing, shallow water and overhanging rocks or tree root systems in which to build their nests. These lovely birds are aptly named as they bob up and down on a rock and they have the strange habit of 'walking' underwater as they search for insect larvae. They seem too heavy to fly and to my mind they appear like flying cricket balls, their wings beating rapidly to keep airborne.

It is a good place to nature watch, and if you sit still and keep quiet there is much to see and enjoy. Dragonflies flit over the River. There are constant rustles in the vegetation from small mammals and bees hum around the Indian balsam that has colonised much of our rivers. It's a promising place to see a kingfisher, and a grey wagtail is sure to make its undulating flight over the water to alight on a rock, wagging its tail up and down.

Goosander and ducklings

Grayling – 'Ladies of the Stream'

26. CROMFORD CANAL

From Cromford the Derwent winds its way in a long loop across its new flood plain, but an equally enjoyable walk follows the canal from its terminus at Cromford Wharf to cross the River a mile downstream via the aqueduct. From this point the road, railway, river and canal are all channelled into a steeply wooded valley in an area of great natural beauty and fascinating industrial heritage.

The canal was originally envisaged as an extension of the Erewash canal but the owners prevaricated, concerned about the water supply. After much lobbying and with the substantial weight of Sir Richard Arkwright behind the proposal, the canal was finally approved and completed in 1794 after many difficulties and much overspending.

Today, about five miles of the canal from Cromford to Ambergate have been restored, providing a lovely section of level walking in a wooded valley. The southern stretches have deteriorated somewhat. The canal has been breached in places and undergrowth has invaded. Canals over this sort of landscape often leaked so they were usually packed with clay on the bed and sides, but this required a lot of maintenance. Burrowing mammals such as water voles played havoc with the system and a layer of stones had to be inserted.

The water vole is still fairly common along the canal, although numbers have been decimated nationwide as a result of various factors including predation by mink. The voles (Ratty in *The Wind in the Willows*) are delightful creatures and seem to spend most of their time munching large quantities of grass, often oblivious to your presence. Whilst I was fishing one day a water vole sat on my foot and spent a couple of minutes energetically washing itself.

The canal and river provide a nature-lover's paradise since different habitats contribute to a wide variety of plant and animal life. Generally, the canal which is at a higher level, is warmer and sunnier and its water is crystal clear and still. The River on the other hand flows rapidly through damp, shady woodland along its boulder-fringed banks. These habitats are just a few yards apart yet the natural history of each remains separate.

Another local resident which seems to enjoy life on the canal is the little grebe, and the ones around High Peak Junction have become so accustomed to visitors that you can observe them at close quarters, even as they sit on their nests. Normally, little grebes would quickly cover their eggs with nest material and be under the water before you could say 'knife.' You can even see these swimming underwater when they dive down to catch insects and small fry, but I've sometimes held my breath in suspense as a nearby pike lurks menacingly in the weeds. Perhaps it would require larger pike than these to make a meal of an adult grebe, but the young are vulnerable – a risk the parents minimise by carrying the very young on their backs.

This area simply abounds with wildlife. You never know what you are going to see next and the wooded slopes are full of surprises. I have wandered around the canal many times, in all seasons of the year and its diversity never ceases to amaze me and its atmosphere is ever delightful.

Leawood Pump House and Cromford Canal

Ashley Bryant

27. THE AQUEDUCT

This painting shows the River as we look upstream to the aqueduct of the Cromford canal. This has become one of my favourite locations and I often 'drop-in' here when I have half an hour to spare. The River picks up speed as it flows through the steeply wooded valley, its course breaking into rapids here and there. The banks are fringed with huge boulders as the River has worn away earth and smaller rocks around them, but I suspect some of these giants were sent crashing down the hillside when the Midland Railway built its extension to High Peak Junction.

Along the River we find the cool, damp and shady woodland carpeted in the Spring with wild garlic and clumps of bluebells. There is hardly a tree not cloaked in ivy, which also covers large areas of ground.

From my experience I have often found it best to keep still, and animals will be seen engaged in their normal routines, whereas blundering through a wood will result at best in glimpses of the backs of departing creatures.

During one such spell of wildlife watching I heard a frantic squeaking and there just behind me were two weasels fighting with amazing fury. They tumbled through the ivy, up and down the rocks; I don't think I ever experienced movements so fast and in a moment they seemed to be all around me, fighting with such aggression. I wrapped the bottom of my trousers around my ankles to eliminate a potential bolt hole!

On another occasion a sparrow-hawk flew along the River and into the woodland opposite, a dipper between its talons. I was a little sad since I like dippers, but the presence of any predator means there is sufficient prey to support it, and hopefully other dippers will survive.

A very significant and encouraging story is the nationwide success of the otter returning to some of its former haunts, and the Derwent is no exception. At present, otters are confined mainly to the lower Derwent below Derby, but they are spreading northwards and are seen in these reaches and tributaries of the Derwent nearby. Otters are very territorial animals, each male defending a fair length of River, and the occupation of new areas is generally by younger animals or displaced older males.

The Derbyshire Wildlife Trust is taking a positive role to help to re-establish this beautiful animal and has appointed an officer with special responsibility for them. He told me that the approach was essentially a holistic one to ensure that all conditions for their survival and success are made available so that when otters appear naturally they will find ideal conditions in place. These requirements cover suitable food supplies, shelters (often in the form of artificial holts) and dialogue with landowners to minimise disturbance and foster understanding. Conditions on the middle and upper reaches of the Derwent are very promising for the otter's return, and I hope it will not be too long before I see this delightful creature's head pop out of the water.

An ideal habitat for otters

28. HALF-PENNY BRIDGE

It was a common practice to charge tolls for crossing bridges, and as the name suggests, Half-penny Bridge at Ambergate once charged half an old penny, which would have enabled you to cross nearly five hundred times for little more than £1. A complicated list of charges was often introduced at these river crossings covering 'people', horses, livestock and freight.

In my painting the evening Winter sunshine lends a bronze glow to the water as it glides smoothly under the arches of the bridge.

A hundred yards upstream the River has been joined by the River Amber, notorious some years ago for its heavily polluted lower regions, but fortunately its water quality is now vastly improved.

The Derwent Valley becomes gentler and less steep as we proceed southwards, but it is no less attractive. I have always admired the wooded slopes between Ambergate and Belper whilst driving along the A6, and the painting below provides one snapshot of this journey.

The Derwent Valley between Ambergate and Belper

Ashley Bryant.

29. RIVERSIDE GARDENS

A leading newspaper recently conducted a survey of parks and gardens across Britain, and placed the riverside gardens at Belper prominently in the top fifty. This is hardly surprising to anyone who visits this lovely space with its neat lawns, immaculate flower beds and woodland walks, next to the River and Belper Mills.

George Herbert Strutt, a descendant of Jedediah Strutt who built the first mill here, provided the land for the gardens, although it was first conceived in 1905 as a riverside space for boating facilities. An osier bed was cleared – the osiers having been grown to make baskets used in the mills, and a boathouse and boating stage were prepared. The facilities were then extended to provide gardens and an arboretum, echoing in a smaller way the gift of the world's first public park, the Arboretum in Derby, which had been given by Joseph Strutt, a son of Jedediah.

People have enjoyed this gem of a garden ever since and concerts and social events have been held here since its inception in 1906. The last decade of the twentieth century has seen a revival to its earlier glory, and the Belper River Gardens Committee was formed to maintain its development. The gardens are a venue for celebrating national events, and like many Derbyshire villages the well-dressing custom, seen here in the gardens, has been re-introduced.

It is interesting to sit in any public space and 'people-watch', and for the artist to make mental notes of shapes, sizes and postures. The people in this painting are not all from Belper; some are from previous people-watching exercises committed to memory, and no doubt some of the Belper population will appear elsewhere in my other paintings.

It is usual nowadays to see boating facilities for the public, and encouraging to find that boats are available for hire on this lake-like stretch of the Derwent. Great care is taken to provide children with life-jackets, and I noted that each boat is shepherded away carefully from the landing stage by the attendant. The boats themselves have an Edwardian elegance and provide a link with the original boating concept of the gardens. Just downstream we see the bulk of Belper Mills, our next port of call.

Belper River Gardens

Astley Bryant

30. BELPER MILLS

The huge red brick East Mill at Belper has been a prominent feature for many years, the most recent in a series of mill buildings which provide another chapter in the industrialisation of the Derwent Valley. My painting looks upstream to this structure, to the front of which is the Belper North Mill which now houses the Derwent Valley Visitor Centre, and where conducted tours of the mill are available.

It was Jedediah Strutt who set up the cotton textile business and founded a dynasty of Strutts who were to follow his lead in developing the business and in shaping the town. Jedediah, a contemporary of Arkwright and indeed his partner and financial backer, was born in 1726 to a nearby farming family. However, his talents and interests lay in mechanical engineering and he eventually gravitated to the framework knitting industry of the East Midlands, becoming a hosier. He put his engineering skills to good use by developing an improvement to an ancient type of knitting machine that had been used since Tudor times. This, the Derby Rib as it became known, automated the knitting of ribbed sections of hosiery giving shape and elasticity to garments.

It is said that success is five per cent inspiration and ninety per cent perspiration, and Jedediah and his son William worked tirelessly to build their business. Initially the Strutts had worked in silk at their mill in Derby but cotton was becoming the new wonder material and it was the development of cotton spinning which brought them into partnership with Arkwright.

The Strutts' inventive powers and advice helped Arkwright to develop his ideas for his mill at Cromford, and by 1776 Jedediah Strutt was starting his first mill at Belper. The site here may have been chosen as there was already a cottage-style hosiery business in Belper providing a nucleus of a workforce and the new South Mill employed many of these people.

A second mill burned down in 1803 but it must have been an accident waiting to happen, with inflammable materials and cotton dust in a wooden-framed building, lit by candle and lamp light. Like a phoenix, a new mill rose from the ashes in 1804, but built to a radically different design to make it as fire-proof as possible. Cast iron was used for the frames instead of timber, with iron ties and brick arches for interior walls and brick floors, reducing the use of wood just to window frames and doors. This is the present North Mill. William Strutt is credited with these innovations, improving on the model of a similar fire-proof mill in Shrewsbury.

Jedediah Strutt was a man of strong religious convictions and remained a solemn, introspective man despite his wealth. However, he seems to have shown a concern for the welfare of his employees and built good quality houses for them at the Clusters and Long Row in Belper and also the Unitarian Chapel. Further generations of Strutts went on to make their contributions; William was responsible for the building of the new St Mary's Bridge in Derby and founded schools in both Belper and Derby. He also introduced gas lighting into his mills and the streets of Belper, which must have given far better lighting conditions for his workers, as well as safety. The Strutts also gave a hospital to Belper, and the river gardens, as we have seen. This family gained much but gave a lot in return; sadly this sort of benefaction seems to have been lost in the present day.

Before we leave the industry of this region, a note should be made of the nail-making industry which existed here for 800 years. It seems possible that impetus was given to this craft when the Norman hunting forest of 'The Frith' was in use and nobleman required horse-shoes and nails for their mounts. This remained a 'cottage' industry until its demise in Victorian times, when hammers and strong muscles gave way to machinery.

It was said that the nailers had a reputation for hard drinking which led them into debt and crime – although the mill workers may not have been entirely blameless in this respect. The Belper Historical Society has some interesting facts on the town's wayward ways and some surprising stories to tell. I expect my own great-great-great-grand-father could have been a mine of information too, since he was one of the very first policemen to have been employed in the town in about 1860!

31. LUNCH TIME

The millennium gave an opportunity for towns and villages up and down the country to mark the occasion with a lasting monument – something for future generations to enjoy. New 'Domesday' books were written, benches and plaques were installed and time-capsules buried, but Duffield's answer seemed to be most praiseworthy. A millennium meadow was acquired, providing a large public space by the Derwent and Ecclesborne Rivers.

I visited their meadow in the hope of establishing a viewpoint for a combined river-church painting as other possible locations had proved unsatisfactory, being obscured by trees even in Winter. I particularly wanted to incorporate this church in a painting of the Derwent. As a local schoolboy I had attended carol concerts at the church, and found it to be a place of great historical interest and a stimulus to my imagination.

Following the Norman Conquest lands in Derbyshire were granted to Henry de Ferrers, who as Earl of Derby built a substantial castle at Duffield, almost certainly on the site of an earlier Saxon fort. The grant included the Frith, an important royal hunting forest, which brought a succession of Norman and Plantagenet kings to Duffield.

With a little imagination borrowed from Robin Hood films we can envisage Richard the Lionheart and his entourages dashing up and down the wooded slopes of the Derwent Valley in their quests for dangerous wild boar or the fallow deer recently introduced into England by the Normans, then returning to the castle for merriment and feasting and perhaps to sit in judgement over some poor soul. The Frith continued as a royal preserve until the seventeenth century but its importance had diminished centuries earlier. Duffield church has nevertheless witnessed great occasions when early monarchs attended services, and over the years it was extended to make room for increasingly large royal courts and attendants.

After this illustrious history I was disappointed not to find my viewpoint. I was considering checking out yet another aspect from the higher ground of Duffield bank when a kingfisher flashed past along the River. No matter how many times I see one it is always an exciting moment; they are so brilliantly coloured they are like flying jewels. So why not paint a kingfisher instead of the church? In my mind one door was closing whilst another had just opened!

It is surprising how many people have never seen a kingfisher. Although they are not common birds they are widespread in their distribution. Being territorial and needing a mile or two of river they keep themselves spaced apart, and even send their young packing at the first signs of self-sufficiency. There are quite a number on the Derwent though, especially over the lower half of the River. They fly quickly and purposefully with rapid wing beats, a few feet above the water's surface and will often take a detour if they feel they are too close to you. At this moment they typically make a sharp 'pip' sound, a rather irritated response like the greater spotted woodpecker in my garden when I am too close to his supply of nuts. As soon as you hear this sound look quickly or you will miss this little gem. So often I have exclaimed 'There's a kingfisher!' and my companions have replied 'Where . . . where?' But it's all too late. . . .

I decided to use a location a mile downstream for the background to this painting, at a place called Burley Bend between Duffield and Allestree, as it is a part of the River where I know that kingfishers breed. The water is reasonably clear, there are plenty of small fish, overhanging branches provide plenty of viewing perches. There are also steep banks for them to excavate their tunnels. In addiction, it is a quiet area despite being on a public footpath.

This group of youngsters is undoubtedly a second brood since the season has advanced and it is July. The young birds are distinguished from their parents by their duller plumage, shorter, white-tipped bills and darker legs, whilst the female, identified by the orange-red under her bill, is about to feed the nearest offspring.

Meanwhile I'm going to search again for another viewpoint of the church and will try both sides of the River in different directions in all seasons!

32. FORD LANE BRIDGE

Amongst some old documents I recently unearthed a black-and-white photograph of the River at Ford Lane, Allestree, taken in about 1960 and from the location of the present A38 bridge. This particular stretch of the River represented the northern limit of my childhood territory over which I seem, in my memory, to rove at will. Even as a four-year-old and before I could swim, the banks of the Derwent became an exciting playground, and I enjoyed enormous freedom and adventure along two miles of River.

I look back on some incidents with a sense of horror. On one occasion I fell into deep water and was luckily rescued, finger-tip to finger-tip, by a girl a few years older. On another occasion I decided to make a 'den' and tunnelled horizontally into the river bank creating a cave about three feet wide and six feet deep. One day the whole lot collapsed when I had just crawled out!

This name clearly indicates that there was originally a ford across the Derwent. A river is always deeper on the outside of a bend, as at Ford Lane, since the current swings across to this side with greater force; on the inside it does the opposite by depositing sediment and becoming shallower and so we have a constant process of erosion and deposition. Typically you may be able to wade three quarters of the way across with the increasingly fast current up to your knees, but it's in the final section that the difficulty arises. When the water surges above your waist it becomes dangerous, impractical and downright uncomfortable. Imagine going for an interview or on a date after a January crossing!

In my childhood a small island started to develop in the Derwent just downstream of Ford Lane Bridge and it was interesting to observe the changes over a period of years. Vegetation eventually got a foothold, which trapped silt when the River flooded and this in turn promoted a more luxuriant growth and a more stable structure; so the island grew, eventually making contact with the west bank. The narrowed channel on the other side took the full force of the flow and the current carved out a deeper bed changing the nature of the River in a process of sculpturing that has existed since rivers began.

My theory is that there were far more 'temporary' bridges than is realised; bridges giving maximum benefit for minimum cost and effort. After all it is very easy to build a simple bridge over a shallow, firm river bed. Stone piers are constructed, then each section is spanned with beams, bridging not only the deep stretch but the river as a whole. The chances are that this type of construction would be damaged once in a while but the effort of repair must surely outweigh the perils of fording the river.

I used that old photo to produce a half-hour demonstration painting for my students, and this quickly produced watercolour is illustrated here in contrast to the carefully planned watercolours seen in other full-sized paintings. It portrays a warm Summer's evening looking upstream to the bridge and is seen through rose-coloured spectacles.

Gateway near the Derwent at Allestree

33. BRIEF ENCOUNTER

This particular woodland – marked on older maps as Holm Nook, provided the most enchanting playground. Situated at Allestree amidst rich farmland it stood on a steep bank of the Derwent overlooking a deep stretch of the River. In addition to its recreational capacity it offered a spiritual retreat that I appreciated even as a youngster. The painting recreates a childhood memory, and shows a pair of swans and a fox family coming to terms with each other in a brief encounter.

This woodland appeared to have been carefully planted many years ago with about twenty species of trees, predominantly oaks, elms, limes, horse chestnuts, beeches, maples and scots pines that shared their canopies to create a cathedral of foliage. Wild flowers abounded, especially in Spring, with swathes of bluebells. A flat, waterside area about fifty feet long at the water's edge interrupts the steep slope, and provided a useful platform for fishing, camping or simply for sleeping out under the leaves and stars. I used to climb out of my bedroom window at night to join my friends and visit this lovely spot, returning home and climbing back up to my room over the front porch before my parents woke in the morning.

A boat was always a dream. As ten-year olds we had no chance of obtaining one but at least we could make a raft, and there were large amounts of suitable material at the council tip in Darley Abbey. Much consideration was given to a suitable construction and we concluded that a streamlined craft would be better than a square, traditional design. So we collected two huge

oil drums, spars, ropes, baling twine and even an old tractor seat, and after a few hours of hard work our lovely new craft was ready for launching.

It floated beautifully, and really looked the part. We were certain it would keep up a good walking-pace even against the current, and exploration of our familiar territory from the River was about to begin. When it came to the choice of test-pilot there was only one contender and our older pal sat on the tractor seat in readiness.

We pushed the raft out for him and it moved smoothly into mid-stream. Our pilot beamed with pride and waved at us and we waved back and everyone cheered, but elation was short-lived as the raft gradually rolled over, tipping him into the Derwent. He came spluttering back in the foulest of moods whilst we were helpless with laughter.

Plan B resorted to the traditional square job, and our second raft was tested, proved river-worthy, and then used for many months to give the greatest of pleasure. It was slow and cumbersome to manoeuvre, but we were free at last.

Some small snags were never corrected. For example, the water poured into the open-topped oil drums when the raft was not level, which made for a quick re-distribution of weight. In the quiet of the night it was an exciting experience to paddle on the River, the distant glow of the campfire Illuminating the faces of my friends. Real adventures these!

34. BADGERS

My interests gradually took me away from the woodland as I passed through my teens but one lovely Spring evening I thought I would rectify this with a visit to listen to the bird song. This particular May evening was enchanting, with blackbirds, song thrushes, robins, and blackcaps – all our best songsters, contributing to a gala performance. As the evening wore on the coolness and dampness emphasised the woodland smells of delicate bluebells, pungent wild garlic and moist earth. Twilight deepened and the bird song diminished, replaced by other familiar sounds of the night. A little owl called from its nest in the roof of a derelict Summer-house and was answered by its mate. Rustles in the undergrowth announced the presence of foraging woodmice, and above the River the high squeak as bats flitted over the water chasing white moon-lit moths. The ripples of a cautious fish were seen then the splash of one more enthusiastically rising to an insect; then occasionally there was a distinct 'plop' as a water vole dived into the River, its silvery ripples creating a wake in the moonlight. It was a night of sounds that were normal, expected and comforting.

Then another sound very much out of place! The foot-fall of someone approaching; moving through the wood with caution. This was worrying – whoever it was at this time of night was probably up to no good; a poacher perhaps with a gun? Might I be shot by accident?

I kept very still against the trunk of an old willow, straining my ears to pick up any sounds and my eyes to peer into the darkness. The 'swish' of footsteps continued through the undergrowth then a twig snapped followed by a period of silence – someone was being extra cautious. With increasing fear I moved around the willow and squeezed into its hollow trunk, an act of desperation since it was always filled with huge black spiders suspended in their webs. I pulled my collar tight and backed into the void feeling the strands on the back of my head and shirt.

Peeping around the edge I focused on the sound, now coming from a moonlit glade. The crackling of old leaves and twigs continued but there was no-one there; sounds coming towards me but no body!

On the point of diving headlong into the River in sheer panic, the reason for the disturbance became wonderfully apparent. A badger emerged into the moonlit clearing by the River followed by several others. They remained there for quite some time oblivious to my position just fifteen feet away. I suppose the wild garlic overpowered my scent, for they were foraging in these plants on the damp earth to find slugs and worms. They burrowed under and climbed over each other, receiving mainly good-natured responses, and chattered and grunted in their strange ways. Finally, they had had enough and off they went. I heard them for a further five minutes rather noisily moving through the wood and into the open countryside.

It was an unforgettable occasion and the experience was all the sweeter after its traumatic prelude. I don't normally paint from memory – I'm not usually up to the task, but on this occasion it was indelibly stamped.

The wood at Holm Nook

35. TRANQUIL JUNE

My childhood home was little more than half a mile from the River and from a young age this stretch of the Derwent became a fascinating playground. My earliest memories are of fishing trips with my father, and of forays with friends to the banks of the River, engaging in all kinds of youthful adventure. As children we did not appreciate the dangers of the riverside and after some of my exploits I realise I've had a charmed life.

I became a good swimmer and used to take every opportunity to use the River as a convenient, if rather cold swimming pool. In my early teens I would regularly go swimming with a couple of friends from Ford Lane bridge downstream around the large 's' bend to the location shown in the painting – very near to the present A6-A38 interchange, a distance approaching a mile.

One year a friend decided to make a two-seater canoe from scratch. Knowing his DIY abilities I was dubious about the outcome, but make it he did – quite an achievement for a fourteen-year old. The canoe had a slight curve to the keel, requiring a stronger pull on one side to keep it on a straight course, but it provided endless hours of interest and pleasure.

One particular advantage of the canoe was the opportunity to explore the river banks in greater detail and observe the wildlife at close quarters. It gave a different perspective, allowing for example, to locate and observe bird's nests that were almost impossible to find from dry land, and prompted a life-long interest in ornithology.

I have included swans in this painting since there always seemed to be a pair on this stretch of the River. They would normally breed on one of the two islands which existed at that time near to Ford Lane, and whenever we ventured too close in the canoe the cob would sail forth bristling with aggression, always guaranteed to encourage some hasty back-paddling!

The pollarded willows in the painting were home to many species of birds. A tawny owl once nested in the hollow of one of the pollarded crowns, whilst a little owl nested in the eaves of a nearby summer house, and a pair of barn owls reared their brood in a barn a short distance downstream. Quite a collection! The barn owls were a particular joy to watch. On a summer's evening one of the pair would appear like a white cat in the dark slit of the loft hole, peering down into the rough grass, then dropping down onto a vole. The surrounding area provided rich pickings but the other parent would fly further afield over to the marshy meadows downstream or even to the rubbish tip near Darley Abbey where rodents abounded.

From time to time I used to climb up into the loft to see the young owls, a precarious business as the loft floor sagged and there were rotten holes through which ancient hay dangled. On approaching the young they would hiss and lean against the wall with their talons outstretched in full defiance! Splendid memories, for the pace of the countryside quickened after the mid 1950s and as we all know the barn owl has become a treasured rarity losing both suitable hunting territory and nest sites.

The evening appearance

36. QUIET REFLECTIONS

This scene at Darley Abbey was painted on a July morning, the light filtering through the distant trees with a golden haze, and the River surface as calm as a mill-pond a few hundred yards north of Darley Mill.

The building of the mill in 1783 changed the nature of the River, at least upstream, the water level increasing by about eight feet. Every August until the 1960s the mill released this head of water to enable sluices and turbines to be cleaned and repaired over a two-week period, coinciding with the firm's annual holiday. The drop in water level was rapid and profound and it affected much of the River on the level flood-plain for several miles.

The tranquillity of the scene on the opposite page was transformed into a surging torrent of dark, muddy water over which towered banks of black mud. The River being deep here never showed its bed, but two miles upstream huge mud and shingle banks appeared, fish were trapped in increasingly shrinking pools and powerful currents swept, scrapped and shaped the river bed. Within a few days the mud banks had dried forming a lattice of huge cracks, the muddy water in the main channels had become clearer and it was time to explore a world that was only seen briefly each year.

My memory recalls the smells as well as the sights. The powerful odour of river mud will always take me back to those days by the Derwent (it has never surprised me that salmon are able to find the river of their origin and may well do so here in the future). In this two-week period new greenery appeared on the exposed mud banks, as the combined effect of warmth, light, moisture and nutrients promoted a rapid growth and some of the water-loving plants established a permanent hold.

Low-lying meadows in the Derwent's floodplain were an ideal habitat for waders and waterfowl. The shrill cry of flocks of lapwing was a familiar sound and they bred in large numbers. Where are these birds now?

An area of about ten acres of wet meadow lay on the Derwent's west side below Nut Wood at Darley Abbey and its disappearance is just one example of many that have been lost in my life-time. This area of grass, sedge and bog attracted snipe, redshank, yellow wagtails, skylarks and for three consecutive years to my knowledge the secretive grasshopper warbler. Between the wetland and the wood a dyke, overhung with willow and osiers in part and fringed with reed beds in others, attracted reed warblers, sedge warblers, blackcaps and reed buntings, and the marshy plain supported numbers of wildfowl in winter.

But what has happened to this precious habitat? It has been covered in rubbish up to fifteen feet high, earthed over and is now an area of dry scrub and ragwort. This is nothing short of a disgrace and in my opinion the authority responsible should be made to restore it. Surely someone should have 'blown the whistle'? This wonderful habitat has been lost – a wetland reserve within the city boundary. It never ceases to amaze me when people are surprised that our bird species are in decline. What on earth do we expect? We really must act with more responsibility towards our environment.

Snipe

37. FISHERMEN AT DARLEY ABBEY

There was quiet concentration on the faces of the two anglers as I sketched this scene in September. The calmer stretch of water at the end of the spit of land is a typical place for fish to congregate – they use less energy to remain in place yet are on hand to seize any food washing down in the faster current. There are many types of fish here including chub, dace, gudgeon, perch, pike and grayling, but the most common are roach – healthy specimens up to 2 lbs. in weight.

The mill was built in 1783 by the Evans family, another dynasty swept to prominence by the cotton textile revolution. Their stately home of Darley Hall had been built earlier that century but has since been demolished. These influential families often wielded strict control over their workforce, one story stating there was no public house in Darley Abbey due to the express wishes of the Evanses who did not want to encourage drunkenness amongst their mill workers. If this is true, the family must be turning in their graves as the most venerated and significant surviving fragment of the once famous abbey has been turned into a pub!

The Abbey became one of the most important religious houses in the whole area. It was created by Robert de Ferrers in 1154, its development stemming back almost twenty years from a small chapel dedicated to St. Helen. The ridge and furrows seen in Darley Park are a reminder of the ancient strip system of agriculture on the abbey lands.

The Evanses created superb gardens and parkland where monks had once toiled; and their legacy is enjoyed today by those who stroll along the shrub and woodland paths and through the parkland itself, as it sweeps down the valley through areas of specimen trees and rhododendrons.

Walking by the River here recently, I noticed a small brass plate on one of the benches. It commemorates the life of Laurence Cocker, a Derby violin maker, and his wife, who 'rested here and dreamed'. This peaceful area and beautiful surroundings could have provided no better place to sit and contemplate. Bearing in mind the history of Darley Abbey I am sure that others have enjoyed the same tranquillity over many centuries.

Darley Weir

Darley Abbey Mills

38. GETTING READY

Situated side by side at the south end of Darley Park are two of Derby's oldest sporting institutions; the rowing clubs of Derby and Derwent. Dating back to the Victorian era they provide a link with the 'golden age' of rowing, which came to prominence in the late Victorian-Edwardian period.

Rowing was a popular sporting as well as leisure pastime, before the age of the mass popularity of the bicycle. Lakes and rivers around the country provided boats for hire, and paintings and photographs of the day reflect the nation's love of boating. Images of these times are still popular today – in a shop recently I noticed Edwardian boating scenes offering a choice from silk-clad ladies reclining under parasols and being rowed by keen young men in striped blazers, to the euphoric scenes of Oxford and Cambridge boat races.

I feel we have now entered another golden age of rowing – with an emphasis on keeping fit as well as providing a major sport. From your toes to your fingers every muscle is strengthened and toned, and rowing represents one of the best all-round forms of exercise in our exercise-obsessed lives. You can row as an individual or as a part of a team, in pairs, coxless fours, coxed fours or eights. It can be relatively undemanding or as competitive as you want it to become, and joining a rowing club opens up a great social life.

Over a number of years the sport has become increasingly popular with women and the competitiveness of women's events has surged enormously. You only have to visit Darley Grove to witness the determination of the ladies as they compete and train.

On a recent visit I talked to a couple of veterans as I was anxious to know a little more about the relationship between the two clubs sited just a few yards apart. It was clear there was enormous rivalry – 'like Derby County and Notts Forest' was how one of them described it, as the clubs fortunes have fluctuated over the years. A combined regatta is held in the Spring over a 1000 metre course and settles a few arguments.

This stretch of river the clubs share, along Darley Park and downstream towards the city centre, offers a very attractive location, and conditions on the water are calm and consistent. This may be idyllic in one respect but at other venues the Derby rowers can experience cross winds, choppy waters, adverse currents and awkward bends which come as new challenges.

My paintings looks downstream on a bright Summer's day towards the city centre. The lattice-girder bridge spanning the river was built by the Great Northern Railway and took the line from Friargate station in Derby to Nottingham Victoria, a line that fell casualty to the Beeching cuts of 1964. Even then a journey along this route gave the impression of being in a time warp, with closed wayside stations and long-abandoned flower beds. On the right-hand side of this scene there were railway sidings of which all trace has been removed to create a greensward and a pleasant walkway to the city centre.

Over the eastern side of the River at Chester Green was situated the Roman settlement of Derventio, its fortifications built to protect the Derbyshire 'lead routes' at strategic river crossings, but an even earlier fort was built on the West Bank between A.D. 50-70, giving a rich history to this area.

Gaining experience

39. ST MARY'S BRIDGE

Imagine, if you would, the following scenario: You are a farmer hundreds of years ago, and every week you or members of your family have to travel to market. You choose to take a long, difficult journey rather than a short cut involving a dangerous ford. Years ago you used to cross the ford but you were never happy at the best of times. One day your ox-cart was swept away by the current and you and your ox were lucky to survive. Everything else was washed away – the cart, your purchases and your neighbour's flour and salt for which you had to make amends. Having determined never to use the ford again, you now use a bridge four miles upstream, which involves an extra sixteen miles on a round trip to market, along roads that are pitted and rutted and up to the axles of your new cart in Winter.

And then the following year someone builds a beautiful bridge where the ford used to be. You instantly gain a great saving in time and find you can spend a little of it in the market tavern enjoying yourself once in a while. All that effort and those awful roads are now a thing of the past. The market attracts more stall-holders and customers, and the town trade flourishes, together with your own – all thanks to the bridge.

I'm sure you would have been more than happy to say a little prayer of thanks as you crossed that bridge safely, offered a few pennies in gratitude or willingly paid any tolls that were due. In our present age when the Humber and Severn can be spanned, and a bridge links Denmark with Sweden we take the smoothness and directness of our journeys for granted, and find it difficult to place ourselves in the situations that made life difficult for our ancestors.

Since medieval times it was quite common for bridges to have chapels for prayers of thanksgiving or donations, and St Mary's Bridge at Derby was no exception. The chapel of 'St. Mary on the Brigge' was ideally situated to capture the devotions of travellers who used the original fifteenth century bridge to cross the River at Derby. For several centuries it was the only crossing in the town. Restoration of the chapel was carried out in the first half of the twentieth century by the Derbyshire Archaeological Society and

it represents not only one of the most important historical buildings in Derby, but a national heritage since hardly any of these chapels have survived.

Elsewhere in Derbyshire the shell of a small chapel exists next to the old Cromford bridge but this unfortunately is derelict. Its roof and one wall are missing, wild flowers grow inside and its restoration is almost beyond consideration.

The Derby chapel was constructed at the western end of the multi-arched medieval bridge, but now lies adjacent to the present bridge which was built a few yards upstream. Constructed to the design of Thomas Harrison of Chester at the end of the eighteenth century this classical, three-arched structure graces the Derwent – unlike its modern counterpart which takes the inner-ring road across the River a hundred yards downstream.

The view in my painting looks across to the bridge and chapel from the east bank and is a much painted scene. The two figures are relaxing at the location where the original cut from the Derby canal enabled boats to join the River for their journey to the mill at Darley Abbey. This pleasant, grassy area of fresh Spring green gives no indication of its former use, but as we have seen many times on our journey along the Derwent some developments have left their mark, whilst others have flourished then left no trace of their existence.

My father used to tell me that his father swam in the Derwent at this point when he was a boy and even used to dive in the River off the parapet of the bridge. This seems a little foolhardy to me, and I'm lucky to be here to tell the story. However, the figures in the scene are two of my sons – and this provides a link over four generations.

The area around St. Mary's Bridge is a quiet backwater in a busy city and an ideal place to relax and paint whilst a short walk downstream takes us to the Old Silk Mill in an area where many mills were situated in seventeenth and eighteenth century Derby.

40. THE OLD SILK MILL

This old building reminds us that Derby flourished at one time as a principal silk manufacturing town of Britain. In the late eighteenth century no fewer than twelve silk mills operated in the town and around twenty per cent of the population were involved in this trade in one way or another. The story of its development, however, goes back a century, and is spiced with intrigue.

The production of silk thread for weaving or knitting had always been a laborious task, and as we have seen with cotton at Cromford, an automated method was needed to speed up the process. In the seventeenth century Derby had established a reputation for silk production and it was time to move up a gear.

A mill was built in Derby in 1702 using water power from the Derwent to drive primitive spinning machinery but it was unsuccessful. What was needed were the secrets of the Piedmontese in Italy who had developed sophisticated equipment for the production of fine, strong, even threads, and were capturing all the European markets with their high-quality silk. However, their production procedures were jealously guarded and like the Venetians with their glass a few centuries earlier, they exacted the ultimate penalty for anyone discovering and stealing their secrets.

Into this environment entered John Lombe, a member of a Derby family involved in the silk trade. He succeeded in visiting an Italian silk factory and was given a quick tour, being hurried past the moving, complex machinery. In various disguises he repeated the tours, then finally dressed as a poor youth he gained employment there on the recommendation of a priest (who was no doubt bribed).

Throughout his employment he scribbled notes and drawings which he smuggled out with the help of the priest, and a model was made of the equipment before he fled to England. His brother Thomas set up the Derby Silk Mill in 1717 and the next year was granted a patent by George I to put the new 'engines' into operation. The Piedmontese, however, had not taken this lightly, and set their own 'machinery' in process. The story goes that an attractive *femme fatale* made herself known to John Lombe, and one evening when his defences were down she offered him a poisoned chalice!

This new machinery took years to perfect, but was eventually highly successful. The mill burned down in 1826. It was rebuilt in 1830 then finally pulled down in 1890, leaving the original 'campanile' which underlines its Italian heritage.

The mill, or what remains of it, is very much part of our heritage, and marks the southern end of the Derwent Corridor for which World Heritage Status is proposed. It now houses the Derby Industrial Museum with particular emphasis on the aeronautical engineering of Rolls Royce and the city's railway engineering.

Swans by the Old Silk Mill

Ashley Bryant

41. DERBY CITY CENTRE

One bright, January afternoon I walked around the Derwent as it flows through the city centre and re-affirmed my feeling that it provides an outstanding landscape feature, the envy of most cities. The view over the weir and wide River recedes to the Council Offices and Exeter Bridge then to the distant cathedral, and the vista is further enhanced by the grassy space and willow trees on the east side. My only regret is the shrinking of the River Gardens on the west side, and the goldfish ponds and statues are but a memory.

In this reflective mood I considered some of the changes that have occurred around here in my lifetime. Any Derby citizen in the 1950s will remember the open market stalls at the Morledge and the cobbled roadway of the ancient Cockpit Hill. As a child there I pressed my nose against the window of Sid Sharrack's fishing tackle shop, admiring rods, reels and new-fangled inventions such as bite indicators, maggot swim feeders and the Milbro-Lesney bread bait press.

Cockpit Hill was home to a great form of entertainment when 'Mad Harry', the king of all street traders, set up his stall. He was a master of psychology, good humour and timing and had the audience in the palm of his hand – 'Now ladies, I know you like top quality at bargain prices so get your purses ready – I haven't got many so you'll have to be quick with these. The very top range of bath towels as used by the Queen herself and I know that for a fact cause my brother lives in London. I dropped one of these off Exeter Bridge the other day and it was so absorbent the level of the Derwent went down four inches…They're over a pound-a-piece in the shops – but I'm not even going to charge you twenty shillings, I'm not even going to charge you a ten shilling note or seven and six. At five bob I'm cutting my own throat and at four bob I'm absolutely barmy – but I'm not barmy I'm mad. I'm Mad arry so get that money out ladies just a few left at …half a crown!'

Instantly a wall of hands emerged as if in salute, clutching half crowns in an audience twenty deep. Harry's assistants dived under the stall, frantically tearing open boxes of extra towels and supplying the crowd who were desperate in case stock ran out, but Harry had already moved on to chocolates 'eaten by the Duchess of Devonshire on special occasions'.

At the end of the day when the last stall-holder had packed up his equipment and the litter blew across squashed plums and discarded cauliflowers, Mad Harry was seen slipping into his Rolls Royce and speeding away to his pad in the country.

The Derby Cattle Market that was situated on the east side evokes even earlier memories of pink pigs and wild-eyed heifers, splatters of cow manure and above all belt and bracered red-faced farmers with their flapping raincoats and greasy caps and incomprehensible 'gerovvereer tha'owd buggers'.

As I scanned the Derwent on this quiet Sunday afternoon, the sun lowering in the Winter sky, I wondered what the children of today will say as they stand here in the next half century. 'I remember when there was a place called the Eagle Centre which had odd sorts of shops called market stalls, and over there were the Council Offices, whilst on that side of the River they knocked all those buildings down for the new football stadium. I remember the good old days when I used to watch Derby County at Pride Park!'

Canada Geese – riverside residents

Ashley Bryant

42. THE END OF AUTUMN

The tranquillity of this scene between Draycott and Church Wilne is punctuated by the sight and sound of wildfowl as they fly between their roosts and feeding grounds in the Trent and Derwent valleys. Here the Derwent meanders over a level plain and passes next to flooded gravel pits, which are becoming increasingly important as wildlife reserves.

Downstream the church at Church Wilne is practically the only surviving building of a village which has had a chequered history – due no doubt to the flooding of the River. If we look across the valley we see virtually no housing development from Draycott in the north to Shardlow in the south for this reason.

In an account of this area one author described the isolation of the church as reminiscent of the Thames marshes in *Great Expectations*. My visits here have always been in the late Autumn or Winter and I also make this connection; I can see Magwitch the convict jumping out from behind a gravestone, rattling his chains. I really must come here in Summer since the time of year can make such a difference. I have sometimes painted scenes of particular locations from sketches produced at other times. It is quite possible – you can do anything as an artist but it is a risky business. Making a Summer picture from a Winter one for example, requires more than adding leaves on trees. The River can expose gravel beds you do not expect, vegetation grows beyond your wildest dreams and riverside agriculture has to be anticipated. I have visited enough places on the Derwent to realise how enormously they vary from season to season.

Here at Church Wilne the most southerly cotton mill on the Derwent was built. This was an early example from 1781, the founder having links with Arkwright from the latter's days in Nottingham.

The last bridge across the River is also found here – a footbridge linking Church Wilne to Great Wilne then on to Shardlow. On my last visit one afternoon in January I chatted to an elderly fisherman who was about to pack up his tackle as the sun was sinking and the temperature dropping below zero. 'Just one more cast' he declared and performed that ritual imbued with such hope that only another fisherman can understand. He was not successful but that's fishing for you and there is always another day.

Future fisherman may well catch salmon in the Derwent if projects to restore them come to fruition. The water is clean enough and there are ideal spawning grounds especially in the middle and upper Derwent – the over-riding difficulty being the numerous barriers across the River. At present salmon would only be able to reach Borrowash before encountering an impassable barrier, whilst on the River Dove, another main tributary of the Trent, there are no such obstructions and the next phase of the project is awaited with huge enthusiasm by anglers, conservationists and the Environment Agency. Salmon returning from the sea will be monitored and if – or when – money permits, salmon ladders will be constructed on the Derwent.

Church Wilne

Ashley Bryant

43. SUNRISE

A short distance before the Derwent reaches the Trent lies the small village of Ambaston but both my visits here have suffered from dreary weather conditions. I had planned to walk downstream along the footpath where I could look across the flat landscape to the distant power station. The cattle nearby would provide an added bonus; 'the lowering herd winding slowly o'er the lea'.

Unfortunately they thought otherwise and ganged-up on me in a disconcerting way. The cows with their calves lowered their heads, mooed and rolled their eyes and I was surrounded in a pincer movement so I decided it was time to move to a nearby meander of the River, where I prepared the very cloudy, overcast scene shown on this page. It is interesting to see how the right-hand bank is being eroded, whilst sediment and vegetation is encroaching on the left-hand side.

My second visit on an even wetter Autumn morning presented a really gloomy outlook, but not to be thwarted I eventually painted the sunrise you see opposite. 'Bring me sunshine' is a good motto for the artist as well as the entertainer!

My journey along the Derwent was quickly coming to an end, but one question had been in my mind for some time and had remained unanswered. How clean is the Derwent these days? What is the level of pollution and how much has it improved since the low point of water quality fifty years ago? These questions I posed to the Environment Agency.

The area of greatest success is undoubtedly in sewage treatment. Legislation and inspection systems have vastly improved matters and are continuing as new treatment plants come on stream. Industrial pollution has dramatically reduced, yet despite high penalties it still occurs. It is not always easy to trace the culprits; industrial waste does not always flow in a regular output – it can be intermittent or just a case of one-off dumping. An important ally is the attitude of employees and the public at large who 'blow the whistle' in

an age of greater responsibility and concern for the environment. Fifty years ago people may have accepted this, but no longer do so.

Unlike sewage and industrial pollutants, agricultural residues have increased. From very low levels they have built up as the use of fertilisers and pesticides has grown. Farmers are now encouraged to leave buffer zones along watercourses; corridors where no chemicals are used. This inevitably helps but nitrates and insecticides still leach into rivers as well as finding their way through land drains and ditches. And as others have commented there is the long term heath risk from insecticides.

Overall, the results are encouraging and improving, although there is still further progress to be made. Words I seem to have heard before in the dark ages when I was a school boy.

The Derwent at Ambaston

44. JOURNEY'S END

After a 66-mile journey that has taken me three years to complete, I have reached the end of my project and the final chapter where the Derwent joins the Trent. The River is seen flowing from the north (in the distance of the painting), the Trent flows from the south, whilst the Trent and Mersey canal emerges from the west (to the left in the painting), and their combined forces flow eastwards; the arrangement of watercourses providing the shape of a crossroads.

In order to reach this point where I could look upwards to the Derwent I had to walk along the canal tow path from Shardlow with a storm brewing and with the prospect of yet another soaking for my pains. However, the rain never came, although I taunted the weather with delaying tactics, engaging in conversation with boat people. One great pleasure stemming from my project has been the opportunity to meet interesting people. It is surprising how friendly strangers become when I am sketching and they will often go out of their way to say 'hello' and start to chat, fuelled of course by natural curiosity.

One boat owner told me that on his retirement he had fulfilled a lifetime's ambition when he and his wife bought a canal boat and spent six months of each year travelling around Britain's canal network. They were now in their third year and every hope and expectation had materialised in their new lifestyle. From beautifully painted boats hairy young men and braided, beaded and tattooed young women with babies in arms smiled and called out greetings, and I realised that life on the canal, especially with the prospect of Summer ahead, was a delightful, relaxing and peaceful one.

The canal itself is well patronised by modern leisure craft as well as traditional canal boats and was a major highway during the golden age of canal transport, helping to link the east and west coasts, principally the port of Liverpool with the towns of the east Midlands and via the Trent to Hull. Salt, which at one time was an expensive commodity, was distributed via this canal system and a bonded warehouse survives in Shardlow.

As I sat by the water's edge on this bustling Spring day it was appropriate to reflect on my journey along the Derwent. I recall the time I sat with my sons by the river's source high on Bleaklow, surveying the wild landscape of the Derwent's highest reaches, and it seemed like a different world.

Clearly the River flows through areas of beautiful scenery, but it is not just the geography of the landscape that has provided such interest, but the people who have made and shaped the landscape, their history from paupers to monarchs, the social history and customs, the industrial heritage, the wildlife, buildings, stately homes, towns and villages as well as the ongoing conservation work and prospects for the future.

I have enjoyed and gained much from my journey along the River, and I hope that through my paintings and my enthusiasm I have been able to give a small insight into the Derwent's special magic.

Leaving the Trent and Mersy Canal

Ashley Brynild